Buddha

Gabriel
Mandel Khân

Buddha

THE ENLIGHTENED ONE

THUNDER BAY
P · R · E · S · S
San Diego, California

ART DIRECTOR
Giorgio Seppi

DESIGN AND LAYOUTS
Elena Dal Maso

COVER
Federico Magi

MAPS
Margil, Milan

DRAWINGS ON PAGES 39 AND 71
Luisa Cittone

ENGLISH TRANSLATION
Jay Hyams

TYPESETTING
Michael Shaw

The text citations in this book have been taken from either original works in Sanskrit in the manuscripts of the National Library of Paris—in particular Ms. Sanskrit 31; Ms. Sanskrit 64; Ms. Sanskrit 151 (in Nepali writing); Ms. Sanskrit 32; Ms. Sanskrit 152 (in Nagari writing)—or, for reasons of preference (for the Tripitaka), from original texts in Pali in the edition of the Buddhist Institute of Cambodia, Phnom Penh, in the National Library of Paris. In cases of doubt, reference has been made to *Gaekwad's Oriental Series*, printed at Baroda and edited by B.T. Bhattacharyya.

For the Small Sutra of the Prince of Hetimandel, the only existing printed text (1938/39), a lithograph facsimile of the original (in the Tar-o Sar Palace), is in the State Library of Kabul, Afghanistan.

The dictionaries used include, for the Pali: Robert Childers, *A Dictionary of the Pali Language*, London, 1875, and subsequent editions; and for the Sanskrit: Monier Monier-Williams, *Sanskrit-English Dictionary*, Oxford, 1899, and subsequent editions; N. Stchoupak, L. Nitti, and L. Renou, *Dictionnaire Sanskrit-Français*, Paris, 1932; and most of all the monumental work made by the late Jean Filliozat, this author's mentor.

Wherever possible—and most of all in the glossary—every term and name has been presented in both its Sanskrit and Pali or Tibetan versions (such as, Sanskrit nirvana; Pali nibbana).

Discrepancies may well be found between the texts presented here and the versions given in other translations, most of all those not academic. With regard to the citations, it must be kept in mind that anyone seeking to learn the canonic texts of Buddhism from either the originals or from literal translations is likely to come away perplexed. With the exception of those books that present only selected aphorisms or sayings, these works are composed of the apparently endless repetition of phrases and concepts—repetitions with only a slight variation in one or two terms in paragraphs that run on for ten or more pages. Thus they often leave modern readers disconcerted or bored. In many cases, when the repetitions are eliminated the texts are reduced to no more than a dozen or so pages in all. It goes without saying that such constant repetitions have been eliminated from the versions given here.

Thunder Bay Press
An imprint of the Advantage Publishers Group
5880 Oberlin Drive, San Diego, CA 92121-4794
www.thunderbaybooks.com

All notations of errors or omissions should be addressed to Thunder Bay Press, Editorial Department, at the above address. All other correspondence (author inquiries, permissions) concerning the content of this book should be addressed to Mondadori Electa S.p.A., via Trentacoste 7, Milan, Italy.

ISBN 1-59223-400-3

Library of Congress Cataloging-in-Publication Data available upon request.

Printed and bound in Spain by Artes Gráficas Toledo, SA
1 2 3 4 5 09 08 07 06 05

Contents

Preface

The Buddha was a historical figure who sought to give meaning to sorrow and pain. Teaching that it was selfish interests and the thirst for earthly power that kept humans on the wheel of life, he sought to provide a full explanation of death to free humans from the cycle of rebirths. The Buddha's original teaching amounted to something less than a religion but also something more than a philosophy. At its heart it was a realistic doctrine that taught a way of life based on ethical behavior, behavior that in turn is based on the total detachment from passion. Thus, there is no god, no soul, and neither heaven nor hell, only the individual faced with him- or herself and responsible for every act in life. Each human is artificer of his or her life as well as the lives to come until achieving nirvana, meaning the state of perfect enlightenment that brings an absolute end to the cycle of anguishing rebirths. This, in essence, was the preaching of the Enlightened One: that everyone can become the Buddha.

After his death, however, an enormous part of Buddhism began taking the shape of a religion. As it came into contact with the various beliefs, rituals, and practices—including magical ones—of the countries to which it spread, Buddhism changed considerably. It took on one or more divinities, found room for the concept of the soul, for rewards and punishments, heaven and hell. It adapted to both the high ideals of Zen—mystical and intellectual—as well as to the esoteric magic of Tibetan Tantrism, all the while keeping alive the simple and innocent doctrine of Buddhism's original monks in the Theravada school.

This detailed, compact book provides an overview of Buddhism, its origins, and all its diverse forms and variations.

The Life of the Historical Buddha

Buddhism came into being as a way of life designed to achieve a rational comprehension and understanding of existence as a means to end earthly suffering. The teachings of the Buddha offer humanity an enlightened awareness of reality.

The Origins

If we suddenly feel overcome by our modern "consumer culture," so barren and materialistic, lacking any romantic or spiritual beauty, where can we turn? Where can we find a peaceful spot in which to immerse ourselves in the deep, reassuring stream of a changeless tradition?

This anxious longing for peace, this thirst for a sense of the divine, often wells up in us—and only rarely does it reach a satisfying response. Of course, there are several ways of meeting the need, and one of them might just as well be, "Why not take a trip to India?" That immense subcontinent, fully one-third the size of Europe, has been the site of many great civilizations and magnificent empires, along with many ideological and scientific events; most of all, perhaps, it has been home to many

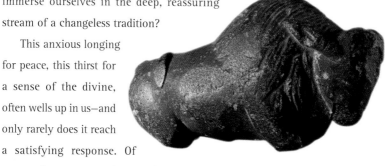

schools of thought and mysticism, among the most important such schools in the world, each of which has left traces of its passing, even though, in the final analysis, one has the impression that nothing in India has ever changed. It is such an extraordinary coun-

Above: Art of the Indus valley civilization: sculpture of a water buffalo in hard stone from Mohenjo-Daro, Pakistan; National Museum, New Delhi.

Below: Over the course of the second half of the second millennium BC, the Aryans, a nomadic barbarian people, invaded India from the northeast and destroyed the great Indus Valley civilization, the twin capitals of which had been Harappa and Mohenjo-Daro (in today's Pakistan). At the beginning of the second millennium BC they conquered the Ganges Valley, and Kurukshetra (to the south of modern Delhi) became the "holy land" of Brahmanism. Various Aryan kingdoms later arose, among them those of Videha (Behar), Magadha, and the northern Deccan. When he arrived in modern Nepal, Buddha gave his first sermon near Kasi (Benares or Varansi).

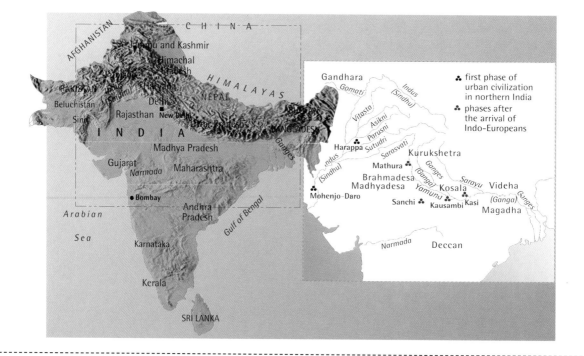

Above: This detail of Mohenjo-Daro attests to the city's high level of urban planning.

Below: Seal with relief image of a rhinoceros, 2500 BC, Indus Valley civilization.

in the development of learning and science.

In a text believed to be a thousand years old, the Ngut Sut Vrvpratthbeth, we read: "Fix one point of

try: fire is still worshiped there, much as it was five thousand years ago; many regions are cultivated using systems that are equally old; and most of all, phenomena that modern scientific and medical knowledge declare impossible seem to occur in India within the normal realities of everyday life.

From the earliest times India carried on cultural and commercial exchanges with Mesopotamia, Egypt, Greece, and Rome, but in our minds we still relegate it to far distant borders, mysterious and unreachable, and this is the case even though India has performed a far from secondary role

a compass to the source of the Ststl [the Sutlej River], open the other a distance of *777 mulkh* [about 130 miles]. Within this circle rise three rivers: the Vrvith [Indus], Patruth [Ganges], and Thbeth [Brahmaputra]. The first descends to the west, the second to the south, the third to the east. None rises to the north, none goes into the darkness. These are the waters that have given life to the knowledge of being and of the future, of the One and the Many. These are the Mother waters for those who wish to drink at the source of the beginning and to know the beginning of the movement of the worlds."

Around 3500 BC a civilization came into being in the valley of the Indus River and grew to become one

Above: Urban structure of Mohenjo-Daro with constructions aligned in a grid pattern and the use of baked bricks for both buildings and pedestrian walkways; there was also a complex and efficient system of drainage and wells.

Opposite: Four-headed Brahma riding Hamsa, the Nordic "swan," his traditional vehicle; miniature in the Pahari Rajput style from Mankot, ca. 1720; opaque watercolors and gold on paper; Hodgkin Collection.

of the most preeminent of the world. It was the source of a certain kind of philosophic and religious thought, various aspects of which are still active and important in our world. This Indus Valley civilization was completely unknown until it was discovered in the early 1920s. The remains of its cities that have been brought to light reveal exemplary urban planning that indicates a particularly well-developed social life. This is clear when you visit the ruins of the civilization's twin capitals, Harappa and Mohenjo-Daro, both of which had drainage systems and sewers that would have been unimaginable elsewhere in the world at that time; their public and private hygienic services were comparable to those of today. They made products that show an extraordinary stylistic unity. Their cities were completely without defensive walls, and this at a time when a city's walls were the primary reality of urban life; there is also the absolute absence of weapons in a territory then inhabited by many ferocious animals, including tigers and cave lions (today extinct).

Bronze axes recovered at the lowest strata of Mohenjo-Daro indicate that the inhabitants imported goods from Mesopotamia, to which they seem to have exported raw materials. This does not mean they were unfamiliar with the techniques of metallurgy, for they made fine bronze alloys, although they made many of their utensils of stone.

Over a long evolution the Indus Valley civilization elaborated a concept of God as the origin of the

Golden Cubit

The cubit, a unit of measure based on the distance from the elbow to the tip of the fingers with the hand extended, was developed by the Indus Valley civilization and spread from there to other peoples.

The Egyptians of the Old Kingdom used a royal cubit that was roughly 20.63 inches long; both the royal, or golden, cubit and a smaller cubit were later used in the Nile valley and by the Palestinians. The Greek cubit (perchys) as well as the Roman (cubitus) was a foot and a half; in Muslim regions the length varied from area to area except for the unit used in astronomical measurements, which was fixed.

universe, along with a consequent dual chain of negative and positive progressions that was the origin of a mathematical reality: God was symbolized by a point *(bindu),* and that point was the basis for the graphic sign of zero, the starting point for the related positive and negative numbers.

The scientific, mathematical, and technical ideas worked out by the ancient Indus Valley civilization reached Egypt along the trade route used for Indian spices. Among the ideas thus transmitted were the notion of the golden cubit, the concept of natural dualism, and such esoteric speculations as Hermeticism. Certain mystical religious rites originated in the Indus Valley or at least were given their complete form there. In later centuries these practices were to be taken up by Hindu Tantrism and Buddhism.

India was responsible for some of our most important astronomical knowledge, for the more than two-thousand-year-old concept of the atom, and for the earliest forms of the speculative knowledge that later became the philosophy of the Greeks. Algebra and calculus are from India, and it was the Indus Valley civilization that created the humble but all-important symbol we call zero. The Muslims later served as the bridge for bringing these disciplines to Europe.

Musical notation along with the names of the musical notes were born in India, where more than two thousand years ago the first treatise on musical theory, the *Natya Shastra* (fourth century BC), was written. The first treatise on the art of government was written in India, in the third century: the *Artha Shastra,* by Chanakya. Even so, India does not boast of these firsts: every civilization rises, declines, and rises again in the eternal flow of life—not our brief life, but the ageless life of humanity, destined to last a second on this atom in the infinity of space. So it was that the Indus Valley civilization disappeared, around 1500 BC. What was to happen much later to the Roman Empire, invaded by barbarian populations, what had happened to China, invaded by the Mongols of Genghis Khan, also happened long ago in India, which was invaded by the nomadic barbarian populations known as the Aryans. The Indus civilization, among the most important of human civilizations, was extinguished in a bloodbath.

To better dominate the many Indian populations they had conquered, the Aryans instituted a caste system. There were four castes. At the top were the Brahmans, composed of the priests; next were the Ksatriyas, or nobles, including both rulers and warriors; then came the Vaisyas, artisans, farmers, and merchants; last were the Sudras, the peasants and laborers, people deprived of all civil rights. It was impossible for anyone to move from one caste to another or to marry someone of a different caste. The first two castes were made up of the Aryan conquerors; the third caste included associates of the conquerors along with important members of the subject peoples who had been quick to ally themselves with the invaders; the fourth and lowest caste was composed of the conquered peoples.

The Aryans had their own mythology and

Opposite: The marriage of Shiva and Parvati in the presence of Brahma, Indra, Surya, Vishnu, and Chhatingra, from Bogra, Bangladesh, eleventh century AD; Varendra Research Museum, Pakistan.

Above: Devani and Krishna, eleventh century AD; Central Museum, Lahore, Pakistan.

religion—relatively similar to that of the other Aryan nomads who later invaded Europe—and the exploits of their conquest were added to this, gradually creating the religious texts known as the Vedas. The Aryans did not succeed in thoroughly eliminating the spiritual beliefs of the settled Indus civilization, and members of that culture found refuge in the valleys of the Himalayas, and their ideas later reappeared in Tantrism, Jainism, and Buddhism.

It is not easy to determine how much of the Indus civilization's thought has survived in the complex mythology of the Vedas, which often present the conquests and battles of the Aryans in a ritualistic "power" style. But comparison of the various mythical systems of the so-called Aryan world with the mystery-spiritual speculations of the Indus valley is not particularly difficult.

The base of Aryan thought is the four Vedas (from the Sanskrit term *veda*, meaning "knowledge, intuition, primordial knowledge, awareness"). According to some scholars, these religious texts, which are written in Sanskrit, were compiled between 2000 and 1200 BC; others date them to between the fifteenth and fifth centuries BC. The four Vedas are the Rig-Veda (hymnology; *rig* means "stanza of praise"), the Sama-Veda (*saman* means "chant, melody"), the Yajur-Veda (from *yajus*, "sacrificial prayer"), and the Atharva-Veda (the *atharvan* were

The Individual and the Universe

" *The greatness of this Brahman Purusa [the universal being, primogenitor] is even greater than this. All this world is one quarter of him, the other three quarters of him constitute immortality in heaven. That which is designated Brahman is the external space of man; but this space that is external to man, this space is the same that is inside man, and this space that is inside man is the same that is inside the heart. It is full [the absolute], unchanging. He who understands in this way benefits from complete and endless prosperity.* "

Chandogya Upanishad, III, XII, 6–9

the priests involved in fire worship, which along with sacrifice was at the base of the Brahman religion).

Beginning in 800 (or 600) BC, various works commenting on the Vedas were created, the most important of which are the Brahmanas, the Aranyakas, and the thirteen classical Upanishads, which developed the concept of Brahman-atman (Brahman, the supreme consciousness, and *atman*, the inner self of each individual human being), symbolized as the "great cosmic fire," the generator of all things, from gods to humans, which are sparks that leave from him to return to him.

Meanwhile, two large epic religious poems that reflected the Aryan conquests of India were gradually being compiled, the Mahabharata (roughly 90,000 couplets) and the Ramayana (about 24,000 couplets). Between 800 and 100 BC the Bhagavad-Gita, "the great song of the blessed Krishna," was

Opposite: Stone statue of Durga, dressed and painted, perhaps the most ancient image of the goddess; Bhubaneswar, Orissa, India.

Left: Marble head of Brahma, Charsada art, fifth to sixth centuries; Peshawar Museum, Peshawar, Pakistan.

Above: Replica of a head of Buddha, Greco-Roman art, sixth century; Palace of the Princes, Tar-o Sar, Afghanistan.

inserted in the Mahabharata. This elaborate text, full of ethical teachings, synthesizes the six major Indian philosophies to create a mystical-esoteric route that is clearly derived from the Indus Valley civilization. It joins the route of selfless action *(karma yoga)* to the way of devotion *(Bhakti yoga)* to reach the way of knowledge *(jnana yoga)*.

incarnations, and actions done in this incarnation will determine one's future existence," say the Upanishads. During the Buddhist period the concept was explained by this dialogue between King Milinda (the Pali name for the Greek king Menander, the second century BC ruler of Punjab and Sindh, successor to Demetrius of Bactria and defeater of Eucratides in 160 BC) and the monk Nagasena. The king asked, "Why is it, Nagasena, that all men are not alike, but some are short-lived and some long-lived, some sickly and some healthy, some ugly and some beautiful, some powerful and some slaves?" To which Nagasena asked in turn, "Why is it that all vegetables are not alike, but some sour and

A CENTURY OF GREAT TURMOIL

By the sixth century BC the complex Brahman system was no longer meeting the demands of an increasingly urgent spirituality. The Samkhya system presented a new concept of the law of karmic reincarnation, a new religion arose, Jainism, and the greatest man of the time, Siddhartha Gautama (Siddhattha in the Pali language), known as the Buddha, carried out his teaching.

The simple doctrine of *samsara* (the cycle of birth, death, rebirth) had become widespread among the people. "One's state in this life is a result of actions [*karman*, from the verb *kar*, "to do"] done in past

Jainism

The bases of Jainism are the Indian concepts of reincarnation, the liberation from reincarnations, and karma. The principal rule is not to kill (ahimsa). *The goal is to subtract one's soul from the prison of the cycle of rebirths so it can achieve total annihilation* (nirvana). *All that exists has a soul; human souls are cognizant, the souls of matter are not. The principal means of attaining nirvana through fourteen difficult states is meditation* (dhyana); *there is then the observation of the three jewels: right faith, right awareness, and right thought, which can be acquired through constant self-control* (gupti). *Corresponding to this trinity of values is a cosmological trinity: the lower world, central world, and upper world, which exist in successive eras constituted by the succession of great ages* (kalpa).

some salty, some pungent and some acidic, some astringent and some sweet?" "Is it not because they come from different kinds of seed?" "Just so are the differences among men to be explained, according to the diversity of their acts, like seeds of themselves, that they have planted in preceding lives."

There was the difficulty that this concept trapped the spirit in a cycle of continuous rebirths. This was resolved by the Samkhya system, according to which the human being is composed of three parts: a rough body that decays after death; a light, invisible, and eternal body that is reborn in the course of the various reincarnations; and the *purusha*, the vital force or soul, which returns in the reincarnations but without being subject to the laws of karma. The purusha can find rest and remain separated from the material; and the light and invisible body can flee

the laws of karma to return to the eternal nature of matter *(prakriti). Samkhya* means "number." Enumerating all the elements that compose a certain concept or fact or thought, one reaches its metaphysical proof, which is the ultimate essence of its knowledge.

Not Brahman therefore, not atman, but two firm and constant basic principles: matter and spirit. The body is matter, the spirit is the breath of life. Beyond the intervention of gods—and beyond the temporal power of Brahmans—the human being can control his or her own actions, thus dominating karma to reach liberation even in this life.

Other currents of thought arose in India between the seventh and sixth centuries BC, although all were based on breaking the cycle of rebirths. Including sects, theories, and subdivisions, about seventy beliefs presented ways to reunite the soul with Brahman; at

Opposite: Mahavira Jina, stone relief (1468–73) at Gwalior, Madhya Pradesh, India.

Left: Shantanath and Kantanath, stone sculptures in the southeast wall of Gwalior, Madhya Pradesh. The Jainist religion was founded by Vardhamana, a Ksatriya born at Vaisali ca. 599 BC. When he was thirty, his parents let themselves die since suicide, performed through fasting, was believed to be a privilege. He then began a pilgrimage along the Ganges Valley, preaching nonviolence, and he came to be called Mahavira Jina, "the great victor."

the same time, in many areas of the north, the noble caste began struggling against the power of the Brahmans.

The noble Mahavira ("great hero"), called Jina ("the victor"), a contemporary of Buddha, preached the overcoming of the law of karma through nonviolence (*ahimsa*, "to not harm"). Actions based on desires are like poisons that by accumulating in a body can kill it. It is best to overcome the desire to act, since according to the law of karma doing harm to others ineluctably means doing harm to oneself. This is the basis of Jainism.

One of the leading Indians of modern times, Mahatma Gandhi, wrote, "Nonviolence in its dynamic condition means conscious suffering. It does not mean meek submission to the will of the evildoer, but it means the putting of one's soul against the will of the tyrant. . . . It is possible for a single individual to defy the whole might of an unjust empire to save his honor, his religion, his soul, and lay the foundation for that empire's fall or its regeneration. . . . No training in arms is required for realization of her [India's] strength. . . . I want India to recognize that she has a soul that cannot perish and that can rise triumphant above every physical weakness and defy the physical combination of the whole world" (*Young India*, August 11, 1920).

Today Jainism counts at least 1.5 million followers in India, although the teachings in practice today are of necessity quite distant from the original teachings of the Mahavira Jina.

Left: Mahavira in the act of renouncing the values of the world is consecrated by the god Shakra, whose regal and divine characteristics are indicated by the aureole and the parasol.

Opposite: Birth of Buddha, sculpture in green schist, Gandharan art; National Museum, Karachi, Pakistan.

THE BIRTH OF A PRINCE

In a far corner of the Indian subcontinent, in the area along today's border with Nepal, was the kingdom of Kosala. During the sixth century BC, to the northeast of Kosala, the confederation of the Shakyas prospered, with their capital at Kapilavastu (Kapilavatthu). As an ocean wave sweeping across sand loses its force, the Aryan invasion had been gentle when it reached here, and this far from the major centers of power even the Brahmans exercised little influence. Here, in the month of *vaishaakha* (April–May) 558 BC (the most probable among the many dates proposed by scholars, which range from 563 to 536), was born the prince Siddhartha (Siddhattha in Pali), son of King Shuddhodana and his chief wife Maya (Mahamaya). Because he was born into the Gothamid dynasty, he was given the last name Gautama; his later names included Shakyamuni (*muni*, meaning "sage," of the house of Shakya), Bhabava ("he who possesses felicity, the blessed"), the Tathagata ("one who has gone, the perfect"),

The Birth

> **❝** *Immense the cortege of divinities that accompany the bodhisattva at the moment of his departure, miraculous his penetration of Maya in the form of a white elephant with six tusks, miraculous the transparency of the belly of Maya that permitted her to clearly 'see' the baby inside her, much as through the crystalline state of a precious stone one can see the blue, yellow, or red thread on which it is strung.* **❞**
>
> (Digha-nikaya, Mahapadanasuttanta, 1, 21)

Jina ("the victor"), and most of all the Buddha ("he who is awakened, the Enlightened One").

The birth took place in a grove near Lumbini (today Rummindei), and according to religious hagiography the event was miraculous. Buddhists recognize two ways to view the life of the Buddha: one with the eyes and one with the heart. The way of the heart accepts the legends, miracles, and deifications; the way of the eyes believes only what can be seen, tangible facts, statements that can be proven true.

The way of the heart says that Maya, still virgin after thirty-two months of marriage, having observed absolute asceticism, dreamed that a white elephant entered her body through her side. Ten months later Buddha was born, emerging from her

Above: Detail of a stone sculpture showing Maya, wife of the ruler of the Shakyas, Shuddhodana, dreaming that an elephant has entered her right flank; Gandaran art; Central Museum, Lahore, Pakistan.

Left: Birth of Buddha; late Gandharan art, tenth century; National Museum, Katmandu, Nepal. The art of Gandhara flowered between the first and fifth centuries in Afghanistan and northern India under the Iranian Kushan Empire. This art gave Buddhism the first images of Siddhartha Gautama, until then presented using abstract symbols.

Opposite: Map of the principal localities of early Buddhism and Jainism, showing the locations visited by Siddhartha, from his first wanderings to the moment of his enlightenment and his death.

right side while she stood, supporting herself by grasping the branch of a fig tree. Included in this legend are the words the newborn immediately spoke, the seven steps he took in the seven directions of the universe, and the fact that lotus blossoms, symbols of purity, sprang up on his footsteps. The part of the story in which the child was presented in the temple of the god Abhaya is in keeping with the customs of the time; but legend seems to return in the report that the priests recognized on his body the thirty-two major marks and eighty-two minor marks of the "great man" and that the wise sage Asita prophesized that Siddhartha would become either a powerful emperor or a great spiritual teacher who would free the world from evils. Seven days after giving birth, his mother died, first entrusting the care of her son to her sister Mahaprajapat, also a wife of the king, in keeping with the customs of the time that permitted the Shakyas to be bigamous.

Taking to heart the prophecy of the wise Asita, Siddhartha's father decided that his son must never learn of the evils of the world since he might then choose the life of the ascetic. He thus kept him closed within the walls of a palace and park he had specially built; there the boy lived amid gay laughter and singing, cut off from the suffering and misery of daily life, ignorant of how most people live. Even so, he was not lazy. He studied the various arts with great seriousness, read all the religious texts and classical poems, and showed exceptional talent in all contests.

At sixteen he fell in love with a girl named Gopa Yasodhara (but the two names may refer to two women, since bigamy was common), and married her after defeating her other suitors in an archery contest. Such events and many others were over time added to accounts of the life of the Enlightened One and are narrated in the *jataka* ("birth stories"); perhaps they should be taken as symbolic, presenting not real events but steps along the route taken by every human being in his or her spiritual evolution.

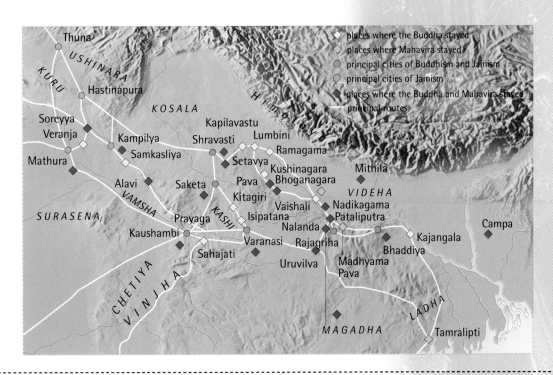

The Four Sights

The years passed sweetly for the young prince in the three palaces and four gardens his father had given him. Then one day, traveling between one garden and another in his chariot, driven by the faithful Channa (Chandaka), he decided to change routes. So it was that he encountered an eighty-year-old man hobbling along under the weight of his infirmities. "Why does that man suffer? Why is he so decrepit?" Siddhartha asked Channa, who responded, "This is what happens to every one, my lord." Thus did Siddhartha learn that all people grow old.

Once again, a second time, Siddhartha traveled by a different route, and this time he saw a diseased man wailing in agony. Thus he learned of the existence of disease. Another day, taking a different and longer route, he encountered a funeral procession and was struck by the crying and the sorrow of the relatives accompanying the corpse. Thus he learned of death.

On the fourth occasion he encountered a wandering ascetic making his way begging, his clothes in tatters but his expression one of serenity. "What man is that?" Siddhartha asked Channa. His faithful charioteer responded that it was one

his sleeping son, saddled his horse Kanthaka and set off, accompanied by his faithful Channa to the edge of the forest.

Along the way he encountered a girl who at the sight of him fell desperately in love and began singing, "Truly happy is the mother, truly happy the father, truly happy is the wife who has such a husband."

When he reached the edge of the forest,

Opposite: A king is entertained beneath a tent in a fresco from the thirteenth to fourteenth centuries; Alchi monastery, Ladakh, India.

Left: Siddhartha wins the archery contest in an eighteenth-century fresco; Matale monastery, Dambulla, Sri Lanka.

Below: The young Siddhartha honored in a palace in an eighteenth-century fresco; Matale monastery, Dambulla, Sri Lanka.

who had chosen "a life without a home."

On his return to the palace Siddhartha found everyone celebrating the birth of his son, Rahula (this was perhaps 529 BC). That night he wandered among the sleeping guests, concubines, and dancing girls, and saw that their contorted bodies looked like so many corpses. He saw the emptiness of his life, the vanity of earthly pleasures. He felt driven to renounce the world, with its fleeting pleasures and superficial glitter. He awakened his father and asked his permission to flee to the Samkhya masters (whose ascetic way recognized the existence of innumerable immaterial souls and offered "salvation from the prison of rebirths"). He caressed his wife without waking her, kissed

Siddhartha sets forth from his father's kingdom to seek truth in an eighteenth-century fresco; Matale monastery, Dambulla, Sri Lanka.

Siddhartha dismounted, cut off his long hair with his sword, and removed his luxurious clothing and golden jewels. These he gave to the faithful Channa, sending him back alone to the palace.

He began walking toward the south, yearning for peace and the truth. This was the night of his twenty-ninth birthday. Siddhartha had become a *bodhisattva*, "one on the route to enlightenment": a potential Buddha.

TORMENTS ARE NOT KNOWLEDGE

Gautama passed seven years wandering as a pilgrim in search of the truth. He spent an early period with a group of masters from whom he learned "theories of perfection," but he saw that this was nothing more than rote learning without spirit that did not answer his questions.

He then went to Vaishali (Vesali), to the school of the Brahman Arada Kalama, who taught the doctrine of the Sphere of Nothing. Severe physical exercise and constant privations were to lead the individual to unconsciousness, thus adjusting him to the primordial quiet of the universe. Siddhartha

Left: Mara's army of demons prepares to assault Gautama immersed in meditation; relief from Gandhara.

Above: Sculpture of Siddhartha Gautama in the act of meditation; Dunhuang caves, Gansu, China.

disdained this useless teaching. He became a disciple of Alara Kalaya, a Ksatriya noble who, having abandoned the courtly life, practiced a learned asceticism (some exegetes claim that Arada and Alara are the same person). Siddhartha learned to seek the truth in the emblematic-mystical interpretation of the sacred Vedic texts; but this learning seemed to him nothing more than a series of crystallized empty ritual phrases. Disenchanted, Siddhartha left this master too. He went into the mountains near Rajagriha, capital of the kingdom of Magadha. Here the great ascetic Udraka Ramaputra instructed him in achieving profound mental concentration, thanks to which, by dominating his body, he could identify within himself the first, genuine, authentic being. Gautama had now become the Shakyamuni ("sage

lasted six years, six long years of privations. According to legend, Siddhartha often ate only a single grain of rice a day; he stood for weeks on end, weakening his body to the point that his spirit wavered. In the end he realized the useless vanity of these torments, as ambitious as the thirst for power, and in doing so he discovered the "Middle Path" between extreme asceticism and worldly life. A girl named Sujata, daughter of a local builder, was in the habit of bringing an offering of milk rice in a golden cup to the foot of a sacred tree. When she passed Siddhartha that day she offered him the golden cup with the milk rice. He divided the rice in forty-nine parts (for the seven successive weeks), ate one, and threw the empty cup in the river; it miraculously floated and began moving upriver, against the current.

Thus refreshed, Siddhartha, who on that day was thirty-five years old, dressed in the sweat-cloth offered him by a dying slave (an adumbration of yogic custom) and washed himself in the river. Seeing that he had renounced his rigid asceticism,

of the house of Shakya"). He understood, however, that the insight of the Brahmans and the sages led to individual sanctity but not to salvation, much less to a salvation good for all of humanity. By this time his great thirst for knowledge had awakened the profound admiration of five ascetics—Ajnata Kaundinya (Annata Kondanna), Bha-drika (Bhaddiya), Vaspa (Vappa), Ashvajit (Assaji), and

his five followers abandoned him and set off toward Varanasi. It was a May night with a full moon. After resting on the banks of the river in a flowering wood, Siddhartha moved on toward Gaya. Along the way he met a Brahman (according to Buddhist exegetes this was the Hindu god Brahma in a mortal guise) who was gathering grass for a sacrifice. Siddhartha asked for eight bunches and used them to make a couch under a pipal tree (a long-lived fig). The supernatural being Mara (Illusion)

Mahanaman (Mahanama). They followed him when he abandoned the teaching of Udraka Ramaputra and retired to the forest of Uruvilva, near Gaya, on the banks of the Vairanjana (Lilani) River.

This pause on the banks of the Vairanjana

sent armies to assail him, claiming that the throne of enlightenment belonged only to him. In response, the future Buddha touched his right hand to earth, calling on it to bear witness to his rights to the throne. Mara, a demon associated with physical pleasures and desires, repeated his attacks, driving forward his hordes of demons, shadows, and fire, along with a rain of rocks, sand, and ashes, such that even the gods that had come to assist Siddhartha fled; but he, "the blessed one," remained motionless, immersed in meditation. During that first night he attained knowledge of his past lives, including the acts that had resulted in suffering. He came in contact with the various levels of material existence, the multiple manifestations of the self, and was able step by step to reach the supreme understanding of existence and reality.

On the second night he reviewed his most "recent" earthly life and what he had learned from its many experiences. He drew from his own consciousness the experience of pleasure, of pain, of mystical torment; of the suffering of the world and what religion had revealed to him. Earthly life is only appearance—it is like the reflection of the moon on the motionless waters of a lake; but the moon shines from high in the sky. In turn, the light that seems to come from the satellite is in reality a reflection of solar light, even though the sun is invisible at night. Thus, on the lake of the human heart are ripples of the reflection (the atman) of the universal soul (the Brahman); when the human dies the image returns to its origin and is then reflected in another being, in a continuous repetition, a sort of "condemnation to life."

After this "completion of feeling" and "completion of thinking," a calm and limitless peace pervaded the third night of Siddhartha. He then understood that consciousness is the result of commands, preconceptions, and illusory notions, learned from birth onward, that construct a false structure around the true self that modifies its essence.

At this point he reached enlightenment and became the Buddha.

Opposite top: The monk Nagasena in a fresco from the seventeenth to eighteenth centuries; Sinon monastery, Sikkim.

Opposite bottom: The three daughters of Mara: Lust, Delight, Thirst. They failed to tempt Buddha on the night preceding his enlightenment; Nepalese art.

Right: The Buddha, seated under the tree of illumination, touches the earth with his right hand, calling on it to witness his claim to victory against the demons of Mara; relief in green schist.

Buddha remained absorbed in meditation. He had renounced everything in order to be able to offer every human being the knowledge that frees one from continuous rebirths. But should he do that? Was it not better to end his existence and dissolve into the infinite transcendence?

He was still troubled by doubt, but the truth was gradually growing clearer within him. "How unhappy the world is! One grows old and dies only to be born again, to grow old and to die yet again, in an endless cycle. Birth and the desire for birth

are the cause of this misery. If one could kill the desire that leads from birth to birth, new rebirths and new suffering could be prevented. There is only one way to extinguish desire: to lead a pure life." Gautama had thus overcome the supraconscious, an entity that is at the same time individual and universal, that ranges at the same time in both the past and the future, connecting between them the mind of the individual and the infinite universe.

Buddha spent another four weeks studying the cosmos with his thoughts, without ever rising from his couch. He later gave his disciples this explanation of what he had experienced: "Holding firm I persevered without wavering, my mind clear, free of concerns, my senses calm, free of agitation, my spirit collected, unified. Far from all desires and passions I was not sentient, I had no thoughts, in a state resulting from peace, from blessed serenity. Thus I reached the first contemplation . . . After the completing of sensing and thinking I reached internal calm, a unity of will, the freedom from feeling and thinking that results from concentration: blessed serenity, the second contemplation. In serene peace I was composed, sensible, clear, aware. Thus I reached the third contemplation. After the rejection of all joys and sorrows, after the annihilation of joy and sadness I reached the not-happy, not-sad calm, the balance of perfect purity: the fourth contemplation.

The Temptations

" Invisible and terrifying demons with fiery eyes, deformed animal bodies, thousands of heads, specters, larvae, goblins draped with strings of skulls, vomiting serpents and hurling mountains, lightning, and arrows (the tips of which, however, break off in front of Siddhartha and transform into budding flowers). "

Oscar Botto,
Buddha and
Buddhism, 1984

Opposite: Gautama in meditation, observed by divinities and expressions of natural phenomena; Gandharan art, eighth century.

Left: Mara in the guise of the "ruler of the supreme sky" rides an elephant in a fresco from the temple of Telvatta, Galle, Sri Lanka.

Above: The Buddha preaches, holding his right hand in the sign of reassurance, while women bring offerings and gifts; Archaeological Museum, Taxila, Pakistan.

Ignorance was destroyed, awareness came into being, the obscurity cleared away, light had been conquered, the obscurity dissipated, while with tireless attention I remained resolute and immobile" (Samyutta Nikaya).

Mara still sought to bring him back to the material world, sending him his beautiful daughters: Lust, Delight, and Thirst. In the pure eyes of the Enlightened One they lost their beautiful but vain appearance. Mara then sought to break his will, presenting him with the frightening immensity of what he was about to undertake, showing him how difficult it would be to reveal the knowledge he had achieved to the multitude of human beings blinded by their ignorance, suspicions, and hate. Worse still: they might use the knowledge to further their abuses and ambitions. Fear gripped the heart of the worthy saint (arhat), but his immense passion for human suffering enabled him to overcome this final trial, and again he touched the earth with his right hand, to have it as his witness. Legend narrates that the earth appeared in human form, driving off Mara and defeating the ranks of demons. The Buddha then broke into a song of victory: "Many houses of life have imprisoned me, and long have I sought the builder of this prison of senses, which suffering made real. Vainly I sought the builder of my house, through countless lives, but now I see you, O builder! No more will you build these walls of suffering, nor ever again erect the architrave of falsehood, nor place new beams in the clay. The building has collapsed, the rafters have snapped, because now I know the name of the builder: Illusion."

And he arose and set off for Benares (Suttapitaka Dighanikaya).

THE SERMON AT BENARES

On the way to Benares (Varanasi) Buddha met Trapusha and Bhallika, two foreign merchants traveling with a caravan, and converted them to his doctrine. This was later interpreted as symbolic of the spread of the word of Buddhism throughout the world. When he finally reached the Deer Park at Sarnath, he found the five companions that had earlier abandoned him and told them, "I am the Tathagata, he who 'has gone,' to teach you first the law," and they prepared to listen.

During the first night of wakefulness, he said nothing; during the second night, he spoke of his past experiences; on the third night, under the full July moon, he gave his first sermon, the First Turning of the Dharma Wheel, meaning the Law:

"This is the noble truth of suffering: birth is suffering, aging is suffering, illness is suffering, death is suffering; union with what is displeasing is suffering; separation from what is pleasing is suffering; not to get what one wants is suffering . . . Here is the noble truth of the origin of suffering: desire, the will to live, ignorance . . . here is the noble truth of the suppression of suffering: give up craving and desire, act with virtue, purify the heart . . . . From pleasure comes pain, from pleasure comes fear: he that is free from pleasure knows neither pain nor fear. From affection comes pain, from affection comes fear: he that is free of affection knows neither pain nor fear. From greed comes pain, from greed comes fear; he that frees himself from greed will know neither pain nor fear. From desire comes pain, from desire comes fear: he that is free from desire knows neither pain nor fear. From the thirst for pleasure comes pain, from the thirst for pleasure comes fear: he that is free from the thirst for pleasure knows neither pain nor fear . . . Sorrow comes from desire. Man vainly attaches himself to shadows; he becomes greedy for illusions; he puts a false self at the center of all being and surrounds himself with an imaginary world. When his soul abandons him, it leaves saturated with poisoned drinks. Thus it is reborn thirsty to drink again" (Suttapitaka Dighanikaya).

Buddha then explained the Eightfold Path that leads to the suppression of pain; it is the Middle Path between asceticism and worldly life.

Above: The headless body of the Buddha in the *dharma-chakra-mudra*, the movement that put in motion the wheel of the law; National Museum, Delhi, India.

Opposite: Gilt-bronze statue of Buddha in the act of giving his first sermon; Mongolian art; Palace Museum, Ulan Bator, Mongolia.

A Lesser Vehicle monk arranging the symbols of the eight-rayed wheel of the law, with red flowers in front of a meditation altar.

Discovered by Buddha, it opens the eyes of the spirit, leads to calm and an awareness of reality, to knowledge, to awareness, to enlightenment, to nirvana (nibbana), which is total annihilation, the final extinction of all casual relationships that lead to continual rebirth. Nirvana is awareness of the emptiness of the smallest elements whose aggregation causes life and is thus the absolute freedom from pain. The Eightfold Path to achieve nirvana is right faith, right will, right speech, right action, right livelihood, right effort, right mindfulness, and right concentration. Then the Buddha explained the reality of the Not-Self and the phenomenology of the Twelve Linked Causes: "From ignorance come formations, from formations comes consciousness, from consciousness comes the concept, from the concept come the six senses, from the six senses comes touch, from touch comes sensation, from sensation comes craving, from craving comes grasping, from grasping comes existence, from existence comes birth, from birth come pain, decay, and death."

After hearing the sermon, the five companions became the first members of the Sangha (the Buddhist community). A little later Buddha converted Yashas, son of a banker of Benares. He was the first to recite the ritual formula (called the Triple Refuge) of consecration to Buddhist monasticism: "To the Buddha I go for refuge; to the Dharma I go for refuge; to the Sangha I go for refuge."

In his preceding life Buddha had reached the extreme limits of awareness. He could have avoided being born again but had chosen instead a new earthy life as the supreme sacrifice of his self, with the goal of bringing to humans knowledge that would bring them deliverance from the wheel of continuous rebirth. And thus, when he decided at the end of the rainy season to go to Uruvilva (Uruvela), he was followed by sixty monks.

The Pillar

" [At Benares] there is a stupa of stone built by King Ashoka . . . in front of the building is a stone pillar. Here the Tathagata [the Buddha], having achieved Enlightenment, first turned the wheel of the law [began to preach]. "

Hsüan-tsang, seventh century AD, Si-yu-ki, VII

The Wheel of Life

The Buddha traced on the ground the "wheel of life" with the three causes of sorrow, the six states of transmigration, and the twelve steps of human existence. He explained that the wheel of life presents everything that can exist and everything that is included is held in the grasp of the changeable.

The term dharma (or dhamma) has many meanings. It is the law, norm, or doctrine revealed by the Buddha, or it is the Four Noble Truths. It can also mean the reality of things. In the plural it indicates the minimal elements of physical or psychic reality and intuitive thought; on their own such elements are meaningless, but their aggregates give origin to human existence, which is the consequence of actions performed in preceding lives.

Sangha is the monastic community, the order of Buddhist monks. The first such group may have been the sixty monks to whom the Buddha entrusted the task of preaching the doctrine and seeking out new adepts, the group that followed him to Uruvilva.

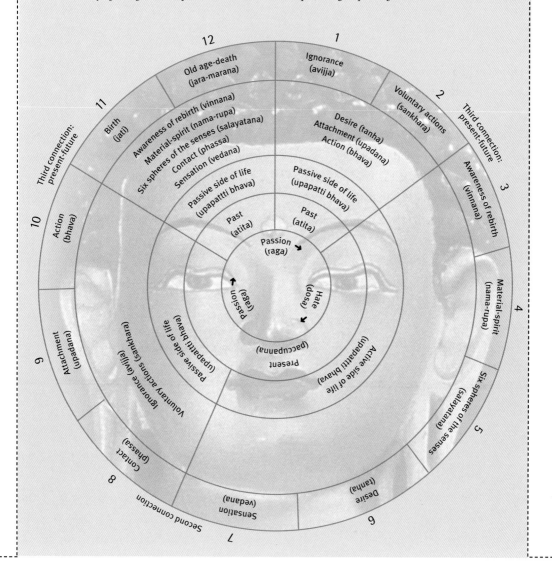

PARABLES LIKE A BAMBOO FOREST

During the long march to Uruvilva, many people came to hear the sermons of the Buddha. Some of his most famous parables are "On the putrefaction of the world" and "On the search for the self." To a group of merchants and warriors who, finding themselves forced to stop together in the same place, insulted one another and constantly argued, he said, "To kill, massacre, wound, imprison, steal, lie, cheat, defraud; hypocrisy, adultery, immoderate desires, greed for pleasures, living in filth, nihilism, intemperance, error. These constitute the putrefaction of the world. Vulgarity, cruelty, slander, betrayal of friends, lack of compassion, arrogance, greed, avarice, and anger, pride, stubbornness, rebelliousness, deceit, boastfulness, envy, vainglory, presumption, and vulgar relationships are the putrefaction of the world. Unseemly behavior, debts, calumny, deceit with legalistic quibbling, fictions, the unworthy and ignoble acts of base people are the putrefaction of the world. Lack of respect for living things, taking what belongs to others, constantly molesting one's neighbors, the cruel hunting of animals, to behave without respect or manners, these are the putrefaction of the world. The wise man watches over his senses and controls his faculties, he behaves in keeping with the doctrine, finding joy in right behavior and overcoming attachment, freeing himself from anxiety. In this way he is never contaminated by what he

The oldest temple of fire worshipers, from which the Parsees drew the concept at the base of their cult; Surakhany, Apsheron peninsula, Azerbaijan.

sees or hears, and in this way he is never touched by the putrefaction of the world" (Suttapitaka Dighanikaya).

The Buddha then met a group of thirty friends eating on the grass. Twenty-nine were with their wives and one was alone, having been with an occasional companion who had just fled, taking with her everything he owned. This youth asked him if he could tell him where she was hidden, to which the Enlightened One responded: "What do you think? What is best for you? To look for that woman or to seek yourself?"

When he reached Uruvilva, the Buddha preached to a group of fire worshipers led by the ascetic Kashyapa (Kassapa), a leading Brahman of the Vedic line, and delivered the Fire Sermon to them: "Everything is prey to flames, everything is burning. The eye is prey to flames, the images the eye receives are prey to flames, every sensation is equally prey to flames. Burning with what? Burning with the fire of desire, the fire of aversion, the fire of delusion. These are the flames I speak of. Those same flames devour the other senses and the mind. The wise man thus nourishes disgust for the things of the senses, putting far from his heart all the causes of suffering" (Suttapitaka Dighanikaya).

The next January he set off with his followers toward Rajagriha, capital of Magadha. The local king, Bimbisara, arranged a banquet for them in the course of which he gave the Enlightened One a park, called the Venuvana (Veluvana), or "Bamboo Grove," and there Buddha organized the order's first *vihara* ("monastery, or residence hall," perhaps from *viha*, "to leave behind, abandon, renounce").

One of his disciples, Ashvajit (Assaji) set off to reach the master at Varanasi. Along the way he met the ascetic Shariputra (Sariputta), who, struck by the serene dignity of the neophyte, asked him the

The Brahman Kashyapa in a fresco from the Tang period (628–907) in the Mogao caves, Dunhuang, Gansu, China, an important center on the Silk Route.

name of his guru and their doctrine. The response he was given has remained one of the canonical truths of Buddhism: "Of all that has an origin the Tathagata has explained the cause; of all the things that have cause the Tathagata has explained the ending. He who explains things in this way is the Great Master."

Shariputra described the profound impression that Ashvajit's simple phrase had had on him to his companion Magallana, and both were drawn to the Buddha's preaching, becoming his two most enlightened and most "saintly" disciples. Each was thus an *arhat (arahat)*, a "worthy one," one who has achieved nirvana through the teaching of the Buddha and leads an exemplary life. In schools based on the training of neophytes, the word is applied to the fourth level on the path of evolution.

Mudras: Hand Gestures of the Buddha in Traditional Iconography

Left: The Buddha gives a sermon posed in the *dharmachakra-mudra*; Gandharan art.

Right: The Buddha in the act of preaching; Xian Museum, Shaanxi.

The ritual hand positions of the Buddha are called *mudra* ("sign, mark, seal"); those taken from the repertory of theatrical arts are called *abhinaya*. Thirty-two of these are specifically related to religion, while nearly one hundred belong to the repertory of dance. The most important are:

1. Gesture of *vajrahumkara-mudra* (or *trailokya vijaya-mudra*).

2. Gesture of "embracing *prajna*" ("awareness"), or *prajnali ganabhinaya*.

3. Gesture of the gift and the favor granted (*varada-mudra*).

4. Gesture of touching, or calling on the earth to bear witness (*bhumisparsha-mudra*).

5. Gesture of homage (*mamaskara, vanadabhi naya*).

6. Gesture of teaching or preaching, called "putting in motion the wheel of the law"

(*dharmachakra-mudra*, or *pravartana-mudra*).

7. Gesture of exposition (*vitarka-mudra*).

8. Gesture of the beginning of enlightenment (*bodhyagri-mudra*).

9. Gesture of reassurance (*abhaya-mudra*; literally, "gesture of not-fear").

10. Gesture of offering (*anjali-mudra*).

11. Gesture of meditation or concentration (*samadhi-mudra*, also called *dhyana-mudra*).

12. Gesture of the ineffable quality (*Buddhashramana-mudra*).

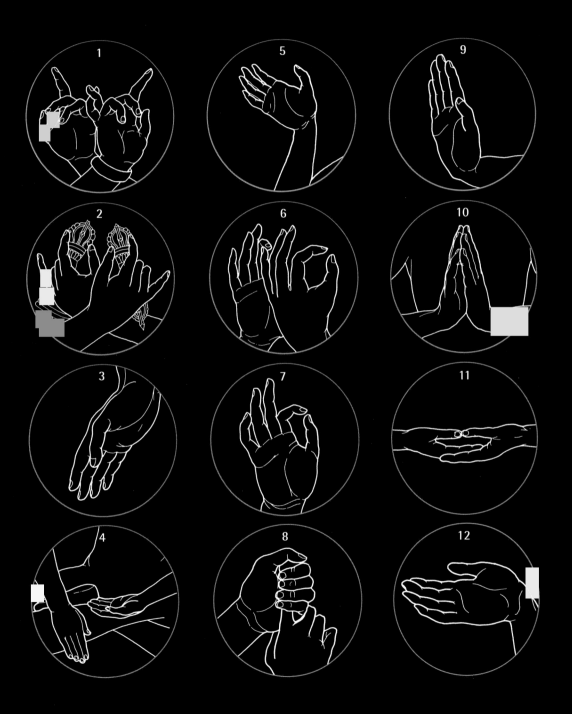

THE RETURN HOME

The day came when the Buddha gave in to the many invitations from his father and decided to preach in the city of his birth, Kapilavastu. The journey took two months, and Shuddhodana, enraged at the delay, did not go to meet his son when he finally arrived. In addition, the prideful Shakyas were unwilling to bow before the great Enlightened One. According to legend, the Buddha was miraculously lifted off the ground, hovering in the air until his old compan-ions humbled themselves, prostrating themselves before him. He then went begging door to door and gave a long sermon, following which he converted his father, five hundred nobles, his half-brother Nanda, and many cousins, including Aniruddha (Anoratha), Mahanaman (Mahanama), Ananda (who became his favorite disciple), and Devadatta (who betrayed him, seeking to stir up a rebellion among the monks of the order).

Buddha's half-brother Nanda allowed himself to be led astray by the love for a beautiful woman,

Left: The palace of the Buddha at Kapilavastu; fresco from the Tang period, in the Mogao caves, Dunhuang, a caravan center in Gansu along the Silk Route.

Opposite: The notables of Kapilavastu; seventh- to eighth-century Sogdian fresco; Afrasiab, Iran.

Fire

" *All the world is burning with the fire of desire, and like every flame also the illusion will go out in the end.* "
Dhammapada

Janapadaklyani. The Buddha showed him a monkey horribly burned by a forest fire; then he transported his spirit to the court of the god Indra, where the beautiful Apsaras were dancing, so he could see how much difference there was between a creature of the earth exposed to the evils of the world and the beauty of spirits freed from the illusions of the senses. Nanda thus understood that all the beauties of the world are of no value in comparison to spiritual awareness, and he became a monk.

Buddhist hagiography narrates that the Buddha's wife sought to profit from his stay at Kapilavastu by sending his son Rahula to him to ask for his share of his inheritance. The Buddha turned to the monk Shariputra (Sariputta), and said: "Receive him into the order," in that way giving his son his share of spiritual inheritance, the only kind the Enlightened One could give him, the only kind he by then thought valid.

Before departing Kapilavastu, the Buddha predicted the cruel death of all the Shakyas, and the death of their assassin by fire. After the death of Shuddhodana, the prophecy took place. The king of Kosala, Prasenajit, was deposed by his evil son Virudhaka, who attacked the Shakyas with a powerful army. The Shakyas, in keeping with Buddhist law, allowed themselves to be killed rather than take up arms. Immediately after, Virudhaka—who to flee the prophecy had built his palace in the middle of a lake and prohibited the lighting of any kind of fire—died amid flames, caused by the sun's reflection shining off his ring onto a tent.

When he left Kapilavastu, the Buddha returned to Rajagriha, where he converted Anathapindada (Anathapindika), a wealthy merchant of the town of Shravasti (Savatthi), who gave the order the grove of Jeta, called Jetavana (which became the group's headquarters), and had resting places for the Buddhists built between the two cities at the distance of one mile from one another. Another monastery was built by a local woman, the beautiful Vishakha, who is said to have sold one of her precious diadems to acquire the means.

The Buddha then went to Vaishali, where he accepted an invitation from the courtesan Amrapali (Ambapali), giving it precedence over one from the Licchavi princes. In appreciation, she gave the monks a palace and a park.

During that same period, the Buddha was asked why he had not used his supernatural powers to intervene in the defense of the nobles of his city, killed by Virudhaka. His response was the Sermon of Katigrama: "He who has a healthy mind does not compete with the world or condemn it; meditation will teach him that nothing here below is lasting except the troubles we undergo in life. Meditation will fill him with such light that the three passions of lust, anger, and ignorance that darken the spirit will be extinguished, and he will enter into the way of salvation that leads beyond dominion over life and death, because his mind will no longer interest itself in earthly things but will fix itself on the supreme good. . . . The chariots of the king, no matter how powerful, will be destroyed. The body too makes its way toward destruction, but the virtue of the good people will never be destroyed. . . . Our life in this world is tormented and brief and accompanied by sorrow, since for those who have been born there is no way to avoid death. Having reached old age all must die. This is the nature of living things" (Dharma Samukkaya: Anityatavargah Pancamah).

The Buddha always instructed his monks not to perform wonders, most of all when trying to convert people to Buddhism. When the monk Pindola flew three times over his rivals, the Enlightened One compared him to a prostitute who beautifies herself to obtain favors. Even so, hagiography attributes many miracles to Buddha; in fact, no fewer than seventy-seven.

THE POISONS OF BETRAYAL AND HATE

The success of the Buddha's sermons and the conversions of kings and other important people did not go unnoticed by the Hindu Brahmans, who looked with deep suspicion on this subversion of the religious doctrine on which their power was based. It is also true that the law of the Buddha, like the contemporary preaching of Mahavira, founder of Jainism, had a powerful sociopolitical

divinities. After all, India had always been home to a large number of espousers of various beliefs, who went around preaching.

The greatest hostility came from the Buddha's own family and community. His cousin Devadatta, after a period as a disciple, wanted to take the Buddha's place and stirred up the Vrji (Vajji) monks of Vaishali, creating a ritual division, calling for greater asceticism and more rigid monastic rules. Using the magic powers taught by the Buddha, he

Opposite: Ananda, the faithful disciple of the Buddha; Gal Vihara, Polonnaruwa, Sri Lanka.

Right: Driven by envy, Devadatta, the young Shakya follower of the Buddha, attempted to kill him, in this case by trying to make a column fall on him; but the column miraculously remained suspended in midair and could not be moved; Gandharan art, Lahore, Pakistan.

aspect: the Buddha was a nobleman of the Ksatriya caste trying to free his people from the power of the priesthood, which had long been locked in struggle with the nobles. Even so, the greatest hostility to the Buddha did not come from the Brahmans, nor did it come from the ordinary people. They were not overly drawn to the learned and elevated teaching of the Buddha, although he had neither accepted nor negated the host of Hindu

instructed Ajatashatru, son of King Bimbisara, to have his father die in prison and then take the throne of Magadha. He even tried to kill the Buddha. But when the hired assassins he sent got near the Enlightened One they were blinded by a bright light; Devadatta then sent royal archers, but while they were standing together in a room the voice of the Buddha came to them from the sky and left them overcome.

Left: Episodes from the life of the Buddha, fifteenth-century fresco; Alchi monastery, Ladakh, India.

Opposite: Detail of a stone relief depicting episodes from the life of the Buddha, in this case his birth and first seven steps; Ikshvaku art from Nagarju-nakonda, Andhra, Pradesh, India, second to third centuries; National Museum, New Delhi.

Devadatta tried to make a column fall on the Buddha, but it stopped, miraculously suspended in midair. His last attempt to kill the Buddha is also his most famous: he drugged an elephant and sent it running along a walled path directly at the Buddha, approaching from the opposite direction. But the Buddha infused the virtue of charitable love in the enormous pachyderm, and the animal knelt before him in adoration. At this point, according to the hagiographic tradition, the dissident monks returned to the order and Devadatta repented and begged for forgiveness, which the Buddha in his great benevolence granted.

Preaching, teaching, and performing miracles, the Buddha traveled the eastern region of the Ganges Valley. His law, the Dharma, was based on the Indian religious tradition, perhaps also on that of the Indus Valley, but he took it much farther, on a route without limits. The actual preaching of the Buddha, the words that his students collected during the first centuries and then handed down by memory, reveal that the Buddha did not found a religion but rather an ethical and philosophical system of life that originally totally excluded the concepts of a god or a soul. He said, for example, "If there really existed the Ego, there would be also something that belongs to the Ego. As, however, in truth and reality, neither an Ego nor anything belonging to an Ego can be found, is it not therefore an utter fool's doctrine to say: 'This is the world, this am I; after death I shall be permanent, persisting, and eternal'? These are called mere views, a thicket of views, a puppet show of views, a snare of views; and ensnared in the fetter of views, the ignorant worldling will not be freed from rebirth, from decay, and from death, from sorrow, pain, grief, and despair; he will not be freed, I say, from suffering" (Majjhima-Nikaya).

What then is reborn? What keeps us attached to phenomenal existence? Desire, with its array of yearnings, lusting, and negative actions. Thus: "After being detached from the five elements of pleasure"—affirmed the Buddha—"from attractive forms, from the pleasures of the mind, you will abandon your home and put an end to pain" in the total annihilation of every notion that constitutes a false self. "As a monkey fleeing through the forest grasps a branch and then lets it go, then takes hold of another and then another, so, my disciples, what you call your spirit, thought, or understanding, is continually formed and then dissolved . . . the extinction of avid longing, the extinction of anger, the extinction of the illusory; this is truly what is called absolute annihilation, nirvana" (Dhammapada).

Was it also the Buddha's intention to spread new scientific knowledge, using theoretical formulas in keeping with his time? This seems probable, since he banished contemplation and asceticism as ends in themselves, preaching constant activity of the spirit and the duty of individual research. But for India the only form of reality was thought, while matter was merely the tangible manifestation of that thought. This can be expressed by the senses, but the senses—because they express and perceive inadequately—cannot furnish a precise image of the world.

The Buddha fashioned a physical science using the materials that came to hand in the setting of that time. He was often uncertain in carrying out his mission, fearful of not being understood and also fearful of giving humans knowledge that might prove too difficult and too dangerous for them. He provided a clear solution to human destiny; our earthly life is conditioned by the body, by sensations, by ideas, emotions, and feelings—all of which are transitory. Such factors constitute life, at the end of which one can reach nirvana. Nirvana can be reached in two ways, the choice depending on personal abilities: for the great mass of humanity there is the path of correct moral behavior; for the intellectual there is the route of knowledge.

Ajanta

This ancient Buddhist center, located 60 miles to the northeast of Aurangabad in the state of Maharashtra in western India, is composed of a series of cave temples dug into the Ajanta chain and is world famous for the many fresco paintings on its rock walls.

   With the southward spread of Buddhism,

Left: Partial view of the group of thirty caves dug into the rock, discovered early in the nineteenth century.

Below: A king and queen in a palace scene from a wall painting at Ajanta.

stupa. The central entry is usually opposite the stupa.

The oldest caves have Hinayana characteristics and thus do not bear depictions of the Buddha. The less ancient caves reflect the Mahayana phase of Buddhism and are rich in reliefs and paintings of the Buddha in the Gupta style and spirit. Indeed, the Ajanta walls paintings are one of the most interesting examples of Gupta art that has survived.

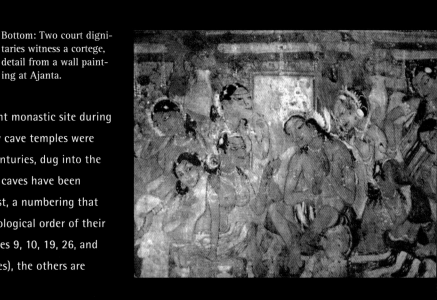

Bottom: Two court dignitaries witness a cortege, detail from a wall painting at Ajanta.

Ajanta became an important monastic site during the rainy season. The thirty cave temples were created over a period of centuries, dug into the vertical wall of rock; these caves have been numbered from west to east, a numbering that is not related to the chronological order of their creation. Five of them (Caves 9, 10, 19, 26, and 28) are *chaitya* (relic shrines), the others are *vihara* (residence halls or refuges, areas of the monastic complex reserved for the use of the monks). In terms of structure and function, the chaitya recall Roman basilicas, with a stupa in place of an altar, a central nave, and side naves that run around an apse, creating an ambulatory around the sacred

A Necklace of a Thousand Monasteries

The Buddha moved from place to place, lesson to lesson, leading a life that was at the same time philosophical and practical, convincing others to follow him beyond the limits of faith while never proclaiming himself a god or the founder of a religion. He did, however, organize his community into well-established religious orders. Without imposing rules—he skirted them without making them clear or abolishing them—he gave indications of how he wanted his teachings to be practiced in two different directions, one for the lay community and one for the monks. On the first, he imposed precise ethical ideas and guidelines for moral behavior. He organized the second in a single community by uniting the various monasteries *(vihara),* but without designating a single leader. That he did not do so might seem odd: as a warrior and noble he was familiar with military organization and the advantages of a clear hierarchy, yet he insisted on saying the monks were all equal. In fact, in a monastery no one was set above or held to be superior to the others in terms of knowledge, wisdom, or sanctity, nor were grades bestowed on the monks. The differences were limited to "masters" and "disciples," the first obliged to teach, the others to learn: "He who has knowledge does not retain a part of his knowledge closed in his fist; in the same way, he who has knowledge knows that he cannot be at the head of the order." In effect, all the monks began as disciples and, after having learned, became masters. There was no reason to see anyone as superior to anyone else.

The monasteries the Buddha instituted still have a clear university character. He looked on thought

Below: The Buddhist monastery at Gaochang, Chinese Turkestan. Ceded to the Uygurs, Gaochang declined in the twelfth century.

Opposite: Two objects of the first historical Dalai Lama, Sonam Gyatso (1543–1588): his cup and rosary; Potala, Lhasa, Tibet.

as energy and was convinced that, like electrical energy, its power could be increased by accumulating it, storing it in the same place in order to best make use of it. First with the single individual, by means of exercises and meditation, then with a flock of such individuals, creating a "working force." If a multitude thinks of something intensely, that something usually happens. Moreover, it is good for humanity to have a certain number of persons embrace a life whose ultimate goal is spiritual enlightenment. Such spiritual research is perpetual, since it is found innate in the world, which has need of evil, both as counterbalance of good and to give humans the responsible choice between good and evil. When a society no longer has men dedicated to spiritual efforts, that society is headed toward its end.

Entering the order the novice *(shramanera)*—who must be at least sixteen years old—shaves his head and learns the ten Buddhist precepts: do not harm a living thing, do not take what is not offered, remain chaste, tell no lies, do not drink alcohol, eat temperately and not after noon, do not watch dancing or attend shows, do not adorn oneself, nor sleep in soft beds, do not touch money. At twenty if he is celibate, healthy, and without debts, he is ordained a monk *(bhikshu, shramana)*. He is then given certain gifts: three cotton robes (yellow or orange according to the location), a razor, a needle, a water strainer, a fabric belt, a fan, an alms bowl, a wood box. He touches the gifts with a staff as sign of acceptance and spiritual detachment. He will never possess anything else. He is not bound by any vows and can return to ordinary society at any time he so desires. Fornication, theft, murder, and fraud constitute grounds for immediate expulsion from the order.

The monk attends two monthly meetings, on the day of the new moon and on the day of the full moon. In the course of these meetings he listens to 227 rules that he must observe and he publicly

confesses his sins. If a monk fails to perform his duties, it is the lay people among whom he begs for food who will withhold it from him, scorning him. For both the monks and the lay people they live among, Buddhist religious life differs from the Western concept of such life: there are no ritual ceremonies, no performances of marriages, no special functions. There is only the veneration of relics and statues, pilgrimages (most of all to Kapilavastu, Bodh Gaya, Sarnath, and Kushinagara), sermons, and collective readings of the sacred texts. There are no true temples. The monasteries vary in construction, from those closed within stone walls, in the north, to the so-called pagodas of the south, which are without enclosures. They are open to all, without limitation; people of any religion can enter them, unlike the Hindu temples, which non-Hindus are strictly forbidden to enter.

Above: Assembly of Buddhist monks.

Left: Buddhist worship hall, or *chaitya*, at Bedsa, south of Bombay. The monastery should be separated from worldly life but also close enough to an inhabited center to collect alms.

THE DEATH OF THE BUDDHA

One day in 478 BC, Gautama, whose health had been declining, called the faithful Ananda and told him: "Today I have reached the great age of eighty; my body is like a rickety old chariot. Did I not tell you right at the beginning of my preaching that nothing resists ruin and death? In the highest of the ethereal heavens, in the heaven whose essence is beyond conception, a life of many millions of centuries is lived, but even there everything has an end, everything perishes. Because of this I have revealed the knowledge that destroys the roots of life and death. Nor, after my nirvana, will this knowledge perish with me. It will continue forever in thought and in performance of the right practice and the right thinking. This is the supreme teaching" (Mahaparanirvana Sutta).

He sent messengers to all the monasteries, calling the monks to assemble at Kushinagara three months late. Then he, too, set off for that place. When he reached the Mango Woods near Papa (Pava), he stopped at the hut of the blacksmith Chunda (Cunda), who offered him some Hindu food. He did not refuse, but that food further aggravated his state. Continuing his journey he encountered the noble Putkasa (Pukkusa), formerly a student of the Brahman Arada Kalama, and converted him, receiving as gifts two rolls of gilt fabric with which he dressed himself. He then bathed in the waters of the Katutstha. He finally reached the sala wood near the town of Kushinagara (today Kusia, in the district of Gorakhpur). Here, he spoke at length to the monks, enlightening them on the doctrine of the order and exhorting them to do good and to constantly search for the truth: "If a man is tormented by fear of what he will experience at the moment of death, let him listen to the preaching of the law, and no longer will fear rise in his heart. . . . After my death, preach what is right, do good, behave rightly. Wherever things are done well, I shall be found" (Mahaparanirvana Sutta).

Ananda sent a messenger to the nearby city to alert the lords of the place, the Malla, that the Buddha was dying. These rushed with their families, rendering honors and bringing gifts

The reclining Buddha in *parinirvana* ("final nirvana"), free of all vestiges acquired in his preceding existences.

To his side, the faithful disciple Ananda, on the limits of desperation, overcome by sorrow, laments the death of his master; Gal Vihara, Polonnaruwa, Sri Lanka.

during the first hours of the night. The Buddha again addressed the monks, asking if they had any doubts about the doctrine; they responded that they had none at all. He then turned to a 120-year-old man and spoke briefly of the Four Truths. Then, speaking to everyone, he said, "All composite things pass away. Strive onward vigilantly."

He then had the faithful Ananda prepare a couch and he lay down on his right side with his head to the north and his feet to the south, resting his head on the palm of his hand, his feet one atop the other, and he softly died. According to Buddhist exegesis he entered the first states of the most elevated consciousness, then the second, then the third. Moving farther still into the kingdom of enlightened consciousness the reached the fourth state, that of the most elevated and pure spirituality, accessible only to a Buddha.

The assembled people, nobles, and monks paid homage to the body for seven days, then they cremated it near the southern ramparts of the city, with all the honors due to a great sovereign. According to legend the pyre ignited and extinguished itself, leaving an intense perfume of jasmine that pervaded the air. The Malla had the ashes brought into their palace, intending to place them in a sanctuary, but the kings, princes, and faithful of many areas claimed them as theirs: the surviving Shakyas, King Ajatashatru, the Licchavi of Vaishali, the Bulayas (Buli) of Calikalpa (Allakappa), the Kaudya (Koliyas) of Ramagrama (Ramagama), the Malla of Pava, and even the Brahmans of Visnudvipa.

Hands reached for weapons when the rulers of Kushinagara refused to surrender the revered remains. On the plain, elephants were painted with warpaint and preparations were made for a siege; in the city, ranks of archers took their places along the walls.

At that point a Brahman, Dhumrasa Gotra, repeating the words of peace so often spoken by the Buddha and calling for nonviolence, made this proposal: "Let the seven kings build seven stupas measuring four cubits to contain seven parts of the remains; and let us trust an eighth part to the Naga serpents [cobras] in the heart of the forest. And let us raise one stupa for his begging bowl and one for the ashes of the pyre." So was it done, and peace returned. The reliquaries were placed within containers of gold and rock-crystal, which were then enclosed in silver boxes, placed in bronze containers, then placed in stone or ceramic urns, over which the stupas were raised. Today it is no longer possible to identify each of

the original ten stupas, in part because many of the primitive constructions have been incorporated into later embellishments and enlargements.

Opposite: The death of the Buddha, Japanese painting at Koiuji, Nara, Japan.

Above: Reliquary containing a relic of the Buddha; private collection of the Panchit Lama.

Left: Finger bone of the Buddha. It was held in a series of seven reliquary containers in a crypt at the center of the temple of Famen (Famensi) in Shaanxi province, erected in AD 147. The relic was discovered in 1987 when the temple was taken apart on the orders of the Chinese communists.

The "Eight Jewels" of Buddhism

Ashtamangala: the "eight jewels" symbolic of Buddhism (in Tibetan *Bkra-shis rTags brGyad*). These are the outstanding decorations for all Buddhist iconography, in particular that of the Greater Vehicle school.

1

2

3

4

Opposite top: The Buddha presented symbolically in the form of the "wheel of law" *(dharmachakra)* in a bas-relief of the southern gateway *(torana)* of the great stupa at Sanchi, India; Satavahana art, second to first centuries BC.

Opposite bottom: The bodhisattva Padmapani ("Bearer of the Lotus"), from a mural painted on rock in Cave 1 at Ajanta.

5

6

7

8

In Tibetan Buddhism the eight jewels are personified by eight divinities. They are:

1. The parasol (*chattra*; in Tibetan, *Rin-chen gDugs*), who protects from demons.

2. The two golden fish (*survana matsya*; in Tibetan, *gSer-gyi Nya*), symbolic of salvation from the ocean of rebirths and pain.

3. The conch shell (*shankha*; in Tibetan, *Dung-dKar gYas-hKhyil*), which proclaims the glory of the saints.

4. The cylindrical banner (*dhvaja*, in Tibetan, *mChog-gyi rGyal-mTshan*), which celebrates the victory of the Buddha.

5. The intertwined or endless knot (*shrivatsa*, in Tibetan, *dPal-gyi Behu*), also called the Knot of Love.

6. The vase of great treasures (*kalasha*, in Tibetan, *gTer-chen-pohi Bum-pa*), which contains spiritual jewels.

7. The lotus flower (*padma*, in Tibetan, *Pad-ma bZang-po*).

8. The wheel (*chakra*, in Tibetan, *gSer-gyi hKhor-lo*), or the wheel of the law put in motion by the Buddha.

The Growth of Buddhism

The family of contemporary Buddhism includes many religious sects and philosophical forms, some of them clearly magical, others, such as Japanese Zen, sublime.

SACRED WORDS AND SCIENTIFIC DOCTRINE

What did the Buddha truly say? His discourses, sermons, and teachings were immediately collected and handed down by memory, during a time in which memory was practically the only means of immortalizing a text. Indeed, all the most ancient literary masterpieces were entrusted to memory. The first efforts to make a written collection of the immense literary patrimony of Buddhism began between 274–232 BC, during the reign of the Indian emperor Ashoka. A modern reader who sought to learn about Buddhism from these canonical texts (whether originals or word-for-word translations) would find the experience disconcerting, for except for collections of aphorisms and sayings, such works are composed of the constant repetition of phrases and concepts. Quite often phrases are repeated over and over with only a word or two varying from paragraph to paragraph and continuing in that way for dozens and dozens of pages. This style probably reflects the custom of rhythmically chanting the texts over the course of a night, making a kind of long hypnotic mantra. Deleting the many repetitions and alliterations reduces many of these lengthy works to a few pages.

Aside from basic teaching, including instructions for leading the "holy life of a monk," the

Below: Memory stick with inscription in Gokturk with the beginning of a Buddhist saying, from the kingdom of the Chinese Kipchaks.

Above and opposite: Large Tibetan prayer wheel in a monastery and a small manual wheel. Such prayer wheels contain mantras, or sacred texts.

texts of the Buddha also address scientific matters. In some cases, as in his discussion of the matter that constitutes the universe, the Buddha seems to refer to concepts that are basic to today's physics. These passages on matter and the atom, from the Sutta Pitaka (Sanskrit, Sutra Pitaka), seem surprisingly up to date: "Everything is energy or a manifestation of energy. Energy can neither be lost nor created . . . All the points of the universe, including the smallest particle of the atom, the energetic units of the elements, and the planetary systems, are moved by a continuous current . . . the atoms repeat, and their endless repetition creates the universes; the universe is a combination of miniature universes . . . The universe is an infinite machine composed of immense spheres that turn as planetary systems. These spheres are constructed of repetitions of atoms; apparently smaller spheres revolve within the atoms like solar systems at a constant velocity. . . . The particles composed of electrical charges compose the atoms; the atoms compose the material; the cells compose the universes. . . . The principle that moves the universes and the beings is energy, the most active physical phenomenon. It moves in waves, from substance to substance. Nothing can come into being without energy. . . . The principal elements are elements found on all the planets. There are four of them, and at least part of them is found in every substance . . . The nature and variety of the substances are determined by the quantity of the particles of the elements that compose the specific atoms of their elements. The agglomerates of atoms in emptiness constitutes matter. . . . There are large and small planets. Some are larger than the earth, have existed for far more time, and are composed of heavier substances that are no longer expanding. . . . The atom is infini-

tesimal. By necessity it contains at least one unit from each of the four substances. . . . That unit must not be divided, but if the atom is broken, the units expand in a chain reaction. The single units

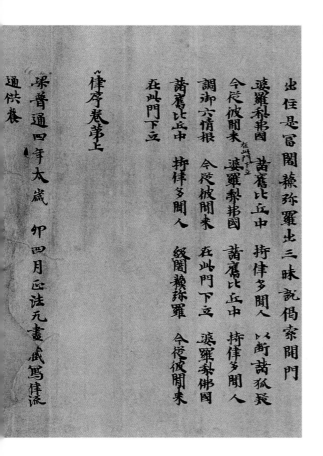

Buddha spoke of atoms and nuclear fission 2,500 years ago. Nor is this all. He also said, "There exists a not-born, not-become, not-made, not-compounded; and if this did not exist, it would not be possible to save myself from what is born, made, compounded." Following the same laws that create a balanced universe, there is an anti-world that contains the "not" form of everything that exists in this world; saying which, the Buddha established the existence of antimatter, a theory only recently advanced by Western physics and still in a phase of development, although it already promises to be of importance to future scientific studies. This theory, empirically religious but basically scientific, was accompanied by others whose meanings have been revealed more by modern physics than by the ponderous commentaries written over the centuries: "Just as a chariot does not exist in of itself," he said, "but is composed of various elements, thus nothing exists in and of itself, for everything exists in a relationship, the entire universe is in a correlation." This "theory of relativity" embraces everything. The soul itself is subject to a continuous variety of states of mind. Our subjective awareness is subject to what our imprecise senses perceive, and salvation depends on the route that each of us devises alone: "As a monkey fleeing through the forest grasps a branch and then lets it go, then takes hold of another and then another, so, my disciples, what you call your spirit, thought, or understanding, is continually formed and then dissolved." And also, "He who grasps causal dependence grasps the truth . . . and he who has understood judges sand and gold to be of equal value. The sky and the palm of his hand are identical in his eyes."

Preface to the Vinaya Pitaka by Zengfu Wuijican, Chinese calligraphy from the Liang period (386–403); National Museum, Kyoto, Japan.

would take on a charge of energy in an explosive flight, multiplying at a fantastic speed and developing tremendous force, being powered by 176,470,000,000 rotations to each millionth of a second. The units would expand from the mass throughout the entire universe, creating a constant flow of energy . . . When an atom is divided into the four parts that compose it, each of the energy units thus dispersed becomes a force of action. . . . Aside from the charges of energy in atoms, there are also those more subtle that constitute the units of the spirit and that are potential sources of energy and movement."

Thus, as extraordinary as it seems, the

The Spread of Buddhism

Immediately following the Buddha's death, about five hundred monks met in a cavern near Rajagriha (modern Rajgir, Bihar) to transcribe the sayings and teachings of the Enlightened One. According to tradition, the venerable Kashyapa, who presided over this "first council," which lasted seven months, compiled the works dealing with the higher doctrine (Abhidharma); Upali, the oldest disciple, put together the rules of the monastic discipline (Vinaya);

and Ananda, the favorite disciple, collected the discourses (sutras). These three collections are the basic texts of Buddhism, the so-called Three Baskets (Tripitaka; Tipitaka in Pali). The first is divided into seven books; the second is divided into three books; the third, the "basket of discourses," is divided into five books. One hundred years after this first council a second one took place, at Vaishali (Vesalik, modern Besarh, near Patna), convened by the elder Yashas (Yasa). Seven hundred monks discussed the rules, most of them hoping to make them less rigid. Another topic in discussion was the way to attain enlightenment and, as a consequence, the qualities of the Buddha himself. The orthodox elders (Sthavira) saw rigid observance of the rules as the only way to achieve "Buddhahood." The progressives, known as the Great Assembly (Mahasanghika), requested a simplification of the discipline, since the seed of "Buddhahood" exists in every human being and must only be developed. When this was rejected, the progressives held their own council. In this way began the major division of Buddhism. The position of the orthodox elders led to the Theravada school (or Hinayana, Lesser Vehicle), and the progressives founded the Mahayana (Greater Vehicle), later divided in various schools, according to their mystical-metaphysical or organizational aspects. The principal versions are the Mahyamika (or Sunyavada), the Vijnanavada (or Yogachara), the Vajrayana Tantric schools, and the Sino-Japanese T'ien T'ai (Tendai), Ch'ing-tu, Shingon, and Zen schools. The most important of these is the Tibetan or Lamaist school, from the term *lama* (Tibetan *blama*, "superior one").

A third council was held at Pataliputra—today's

Patna, near Kasi (Benares)—and a fourth was held in the same place during the reign of the Mauryan emperor Ashoka in the third century BC (in 244 or 243 BC). It was presided over by Tissa Moggaliputta.

Ashoka, one of the most noble and interesting figures in the history of India, was the grandson of Chandragupta Maurya, the leader who, on the death of Alexander the Great, had defeated the Greek forces still in India, laying the basis for the empire that Ashoka, who took the throne in 274 BC,

Right: The large Stupa 3 of the Nalanda monastery in Bihar, India, seventh century.

Below: Image of Buddha, Gandharan art; Museum of Mathura, Uttar Pradesh, India.

Opposite: Map of the places of the spread of Hinayana, Mahayana, and Tantric or Tibetan Buddhism.

enlarged and made even more famous. Ashoka can be considered the "Constantine" of Buddhism: at the conclusion of the bloody battle of Kalinga, with which he ended enemy resistance, he stood atop a hill and contemplated the corpse-strewn battlefield. The despair he sensed at the sea of blood turned him to Buddhism. He converted and had Buddhism preached "in the four corners of the world." From a religion of northern India, Buddhism spread to become "universal." It was during this period that the Three Baskets (Tripitaka) were written down, in Pali (the language of the Buddha, similar to Sanskrit but much less ductile).

Ashoka had hospitals, wells, cisterns, roads, and monasteries built throughout his vast empire. He also had majestic

stupa shrines erected, giving considerable impulse to the arts. He sent missionaries to Syria and Egypt, to Cyrene in North Africa, to Macedonia, to Epirus, and most of all to Ceylon, entrusting the guidance of this mission to his son Mahendra (Mahinda). Buddhist missionaries reached all the way to Rome, Gaul, and England. Echoes of their preaching can be discerned in texts of the Greek and Roman philosophers, in the works of the Neo-Platonists, and most of all in those of the early Christians.

Two hundred years later, in the first century BC, the land to the north of India, ruled by King Menander (the Greek known as Milinda in Pali), a fervent Buddhist, was invaded by Turkish people, the Kushans. Their greatest king, Kaniska (AD 78–103),

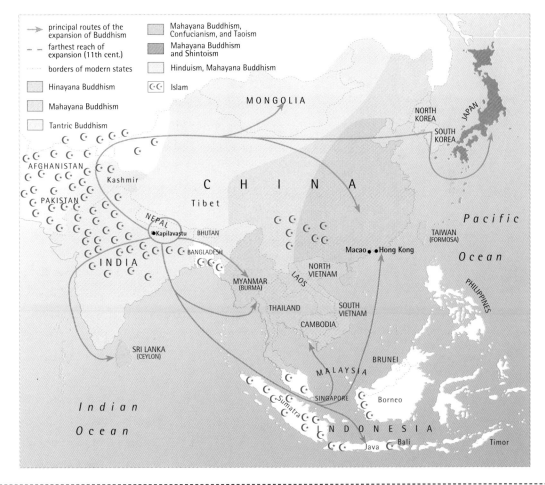

an emulator of Ashoka, summoned the fourth council, at Jalandhara in the Punjab and at Kundalavana in Kashmir, with the declared intention of reconciling the three major divisions of Buddhism. He hoped to base this unity on the doctrines of the Majasanghika school, at the time the most widespread and popular of the schools, but only the Sarvastivadin (a branch of the Hinayana), the Tibetans, and the Chinese participated in the council. The Kushans, and most of all King Kaniska, were responsible for the development of an extraordinarily beautiful style of Buddhist art in the region of Gandhara, between Afghanistan and Pakistan. This Gandharan art was based on Greco-Roman models that had been in the area since the time of Alexander the Great and were still arriving along the China-Rome trade routes. This art provided the basic sacred iconography of all Buddhism, and its models (carried to the Far East by "missionaries" taught in the monasteries of the Bamiyan valley) were at the base of Chinese, Indochinese, and Japanese Buddhist iconography. Chinese Buddhists had attended Kaniska's council, and Buddhism had spread to China as early as the first century AD, but it went through its period of greatest development there between the fifth and sixth centuries, during the reigns of the Turkic people known as the Toba (North China). Buddhism took hold in Vietnam in 220 and a little less than a hundred years later in Korea, from where it spread almost immediately to Japan. It became the state religion of Japan in 610, with the support of the shoguns (military governors) and remained so throughout the

Left: Ivory carving depicting female beauty, Gandharan art; Italian Institute for the Middle and Far East, Rome. Opposite: The colossal Buddha of Bamiyan, 175 feet high. The Enlightened One is presented with his right hand raised in the gesture of reassurance (abhaya-mudra), while his left holds an edge of his robe.

period of their power and until the beginning of the last century. During the same time it arrived in Burma (Myanmar), where it is still the official religion. In 650 the first Buddhist temple was built in Tibet, and from there Buddhism arrived in Mongolia about a thousand years later. The slow decline of Buddhism in India began in the seventh century, a result of both the renewal of Hinduism and the spread of Islam.

The Largest Stone Statue in the World

The region of Gandhara is today between Afghanistan and Pakistan. Ancient Afghanistan was a territory of cultural exchange, from Alexandrian Greek art to that of Imperial Rome, with model examples in the sites of Mundigak, Begram, Hadhdha, Shuturak, Fundukistan, Taxila, and in particular Bamiyan; the region was also affected by the classical styles of Parthian and Sassanian Iran and those of Roman Syria. An obligatory stop on the great caravan route across the Hindu Kush, the Bamiyan valley was the site of many Buddhist monasteries and seminaries. Between the second and eighth centuries AD Buddhist missionaries set off from the valley on journeys to India, China, and Japan, thus spreading a typical Buddhist iconography that revealed its derivation from classical Greco-Roman models: the Buddha wrapped in a Roman cloak, ovoid decorations, Corinthian molding, trabeations with metopes and triglyphs, composite capitals. This was in part the result of the Silk Route, which connected the Roman Mediterranean to Tang China.

Buddhist monks dug numerous cells into the rock wall at the end of the val-

ley and also carved various statues of the Buddha, some of them 100 feet high (second to third centuries) and one colossal one (sixth century) that is 175 feet high. Some of his drapery was made by covering heavy cords with plaster; the face, originally made of gilt wood, was destroyed by Islamic "iconoclasts" in the ninth century. Some parts (the legs and hands) were made of plaster secured to the wall with beams (the square holes into which the beams were inserted are still visible in the rock wall); the plaster crumbled away over the course of the first four hundred years. Seventeenth-century French travelers wrote about seeing the "Grand Buddha" in the valley of Bamiyan, and its image was made known in the nineteenth century by prints made during the two English invasions of the area (1842 and 1879); it was reproduced in photographs early in the reign of King Habib Allah (1907).

The author visited the site in 1938 and again in August 2000 and was struck by its majestic serenity. In March 2001, the statue was demolished by Islamic fundamentalists of the Taliban movement.

THE IMPORTANCE OF THE SILK ROUTE

The heart of the vast central Asian world was crossed from China to Mediterranean Anatolia by a broad river of people: the Turks. Turkic peoples displayed an interest in all forms of religion, and just as they assimilated and reworked the many kinds of art that reached them from Rome and from China, they also assimilated the various religions and philosophical doctrines that came their way, including Buddhism. Thus, Buddhism was spread

expressed in the coordination of its well-organized and powerful monastic movement. It is possible that when the Turkic intellectuals later went from Buddhism to Islam, the Buddhist monastic class flowed into what came to be called Islamic "monasticism," meaning Sufism, the most mystical and elevated part of Islam, which has given many poets and scientists to both Islam and the world. A Muslim mystical movement, the Kalandariyya Sufi order, which probably arose in the ninth century as a result of the Malamatiyya ("the blamers," a Muslim ascetic

into Chinese territory by Turkic peoples, in particular the Toba who took the name Wei (386–551) and ruled North China. There were more than 1,300 pagodas in Luoyang, capital of the Wei, and on the orders of Thopa Hong II (471–499), the Longmen caves were created. These are masterpieces of Buddhist art based on Greco-Roman inspiration, following models imported from Gandhara.

An elitist religion, Buddhism was most clearly

movement), became established in Khorasan early in the eleventh century and attracted many Buddhist monks. In the thirteenth century, this order was particularly influenced by Buddhism and only after its spread to the West by Savi (ca. 1144–1232) did it come into full agreement with Islamic law.

Those who have investigated Buddhism and Sufism have overlooked an important factor within the vast territory of central Asia: the Silk Route, the trade road that connected China to the Mediter-

The Seljuk Turks were of great importance in this regard since they organized the great artery, establishing a series of caravansaries (inns) along its entire route. Most of these constructions, made of stone or brick, were built by master engineers belonging to Sufi orders. Some of these highly functional complexes were quite impressive, with splendid architecture. They were not just for caravans: wayfarers, scholars, students, and missionaries of all nationalities and religions (including Buddhist monks and Sufi mystics) could spend three days for free (and left epigraphs carved in the entry portals). The famous traveler Marco Polo made use of such waystations.

ranean and was run by central Asian Turks. The route is named for the Chinese silk that was among the most important goods moving westward; there were also Arabian incense and precious stones, fabrics, and spices from India. Currency to pay for these goods was the primary valuable moving east, but there was also Roman tin, lead, and copper as well as glass and pottery. This important means of spreading goods also spread culture and ideas, carrying Buddhism to Muslim lands and taking Islam into non-Muslim regions.

Caravansaries were thus centers of cultural exchange; some even had libraries. In the evening the guests engaged in discussions, including philosophical ones, and the many cultures that gravitated around the Turkish states and those from beyond met there and were enriched by the encounters. This essential aspect of Euro-Asiatic culture was among the most important means of spreading Buddhism.

Opposite: The Vairochana Buddha, rock sculpture from 672–675 in Luoyang, Honan, China.

Top: The great Buddha of the Mogao caves, Dunhuang, Gansu, a locality along the Silk route.

Right: Silk Route caravansary of Kanlong, Kashgar, Xinjiang, China.

Ancient Wisdom, New Interpretations

As it spread beyond the Ganges Valley, the word of the Enlightened One came in contact with different cultures and customs, results of the variety of ethnic groups and living conditions in India. For example, the people of the south, given to a more quiet life and not drawn to philosophical argument, were not effected by doctrinal disputes and maintained the bases of the Dharma in a kind of primeval genuineness. Other peoples proved unable to completely surrender their age-old mythologies and inserted their demons and legends into Buddhism. Important changes came about from the contact of Buddhist doctrine with large populations of peoples less sophisticated than the original Buddhists.

The result was a variety of concepts and adaptations of Buddhism, with sects and beliefs sometimes in open disagreement. The geographic spread subjected the Dharma to the same mutability to which the Buddha taught that all things of the world were prey. It also forced numerous centers that had been abandoned or cut off from the common center by political events to evolve autonomously. The changes were similar to those that occur to a core language as it is slowly lost in the rivulets of new languages derived from it, in the dialects based on it, in various philological "mutations." An example is the many languages derived from Latin, itself a result of changes derived from Sanskrit.

In the broadest sense, Buddhism divided in three large schools: Theravada, Mahayana, and Vajrayana. The subtle differences among the three resulted from either the figure of the Buddha (and important moments of his life) or the words of the Buddha and his doctrine. The Theravada school strived to keep Buddhist iconography within strictly contained formal limits. Such was not the case with the Mahayana and Vajrayana schools, in which the divinization of the Buddha and the multiplication of images was further enlarged by divinized representations—personifications—of the Buddha's actions and thoughts.

Illustrations based on Buddhist lore turned first

Left: Avalokiteshvara, "the lord who looks down in compassion"; fifteenth-century Nepalese bronze.

Opposite: Buddha in classical Roman-Iranian dress in a wall painting in the Bamiyan valley, Afghanistan.

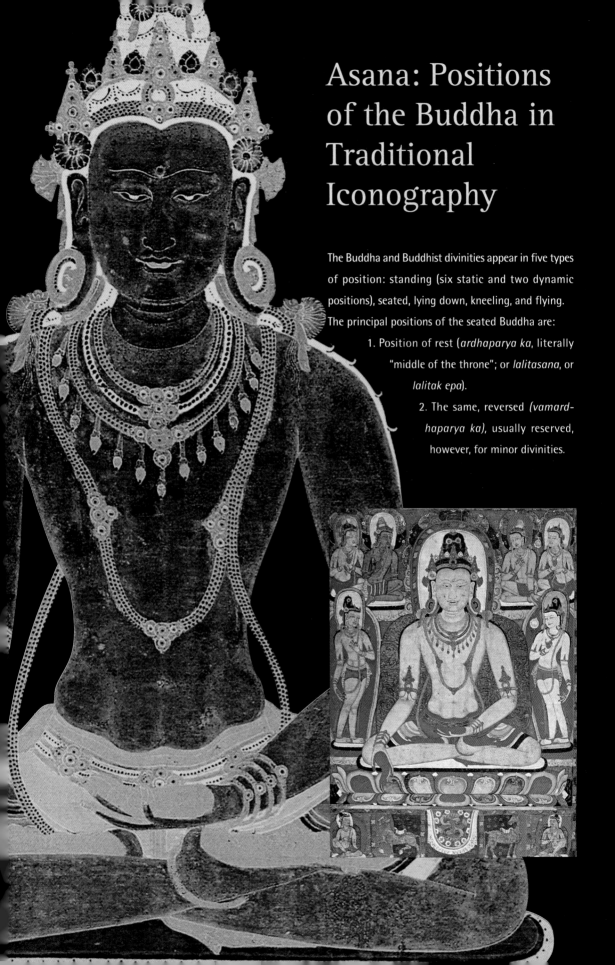

Asana: Positions of the Buddha in Traditional Iconography

The Buddha and Buddhist divinities appear in five types of position: standing (six static and two dynamic positions), seated, lying down, kneeling, and flying. The principal positions of the seated Buddha are:

1. Position of rest (*ardhaparya ka*, literally "middle of the throne"; or *lalitasana*, or *lalitak epa*).

2. The same, reversed *(vamardhaparya ka)*, usually reserved, however, for minor divinities.

3. The noble position *(sattvaparyanka)*.

4. The diamond, lightning, or lotus position *(vajraparyanka, or vajrasana, or padmasana)*.

5. The position of regal rest *(maharajalilasana)*.

6. The teaching position: *utku akasana*, highly rare for the Buddha and most often applied to Uluki, a ferocious divinity, a sort of Fury in the Tibetan pantheon; also used for masters in the act of preaching.

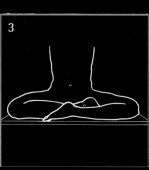

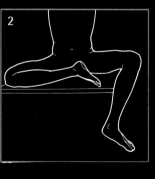

Above: Red sandstone seated Buddha, 27 in. high, Kushana art, first century AD; Archaeological Museum, Mathura. The Buddha assumes the *ahaya-mudra*, the position of reassurance, under the Bodhi tree.

Opposite: The celestial Buddha Ratnasambhava, Kadampa monastery, central Tibet, thirteenth century.

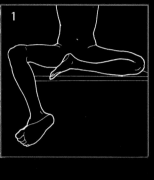

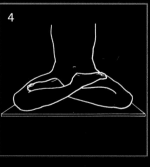

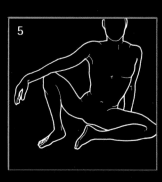

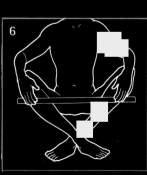

Manjushri, the bodhisattva of wisdom. He is an expression of compassion and presents a serene and peaceful expression—despite the sword in his right hand that is used to cut away such obstacles as ignorance and delusion. The book that he keeps in balance on the lotus flower is the Sutra of the Perfection of Wisdom, an important Buddhist text; eighteenth-century Mongolian art; Fine Arts Museum, Ulan Bator, Mongolia.

to the various moments in the life of the Buddha (his birth, the Four Sights, the "going forth," meditation, enlightenment, the first turning of the Dharma wheel, and his death—to cite the main ones). Each was presented in specific postures within a rigidly formalized iconography. The Buddha thus acquired three basic bodies *(trikaya)*: the body with which he came to earth (*nirmanakaya*, the "emanation body," the body of his manifestations, the visible, historical body of Siddhartha Gautama); his spiritual body (*sambhogakaya*, or "enjoyment body," "body of bliss," expressing an essential quality or level of awareness of the bodhisattva before incarnation); and his "truth body" *(dharmakaya)*: an essential aspect of the Dharma, a specific condition for knowing or preaching the law. These are the three perceptible and concrete realities of the Buddha. These bodies later became individual and subjective.

There is then the mythological Buddha, the "always existing," the Amida Buddha, the spiritual principle of the nature of the Buddha worshiped in particular by the Pure Land school. Its meditation led to the creation of the five *dhyanibuddha*, or transcendent Buddhas: Akshobhya ("the imperturbable"), lord of the thinkable; Amitabha ("infinite light"), lord of the lotus flower; Amoghasiddha ("infallible power; he who succeeds"); Ratnasambhava ("born from a jewel"); and Vairochana ("the enlightener," the most important of the five). The first four preside over the four points of the compass, the last rules the zenith. Based on these five dhyanibuddha are the five *dhyanibodhisattva*: that which proceeds from Amitabha is the Buddha Avalokiteshvara ("the lord that looks from above"). His created body is Siddhartha Gautama, and his role is to welcome souls, which is why he is sometimes presented in the guise of a woman holding a child in her arms. When Chinese ivory statues of him arrived in France during the thirteenth century, they were taken for presentations of the Virgin and Child. The *déhanché* line of Loire Valley statues is derived from the curving line (as curving as elephant tusks) of these carvings.

Highly venerated among the numerous future Buddhas is Maitreya ("the benevolent"), to whom the wise Kashyapa gave the guise and the powers of the Shakyamuni. It is said that he will return to the earth about 2,500 years from now, in a family of Brahmans. Tibetan Buddhists claim he resides

Vajrabhairava, a ferocious divinity that often appears in Nepalese, Tibetan, and Mongolian traditional art. Also called Mahavajrabhairava and, in Nepalese, Mahisa-samvara (the Samvara with the buffalo head, since its primary face is taurine). Black or blue, it has nine faces, thirty-four arms, sixteen feet, and embraces a *prajna*. Its cloven hooves trample various people and animals. The divinity is sometimes identified with Kubera (or Kuvera), leader of the Yaksa and guardian of space; sixteenth-century Tibetan *thangka* (votive hanging); Sakapa monastery, central Tibet.

in Tusita (Tushita) heaven. There are from four to thirty-two Buddhas of the past, according to the school. The number of Buddhas that have descended to the earth—as prophets preaching various religions—ranges from fifty-six to one hundred, but the first was Dryankara. By far the richest pantheon is found among the Tantric Buddhists of Tibet.

As the figure-symbols of historical Buddhas multiplied, so too did Buddhist texts: commentators, essayists, exegetes, and popularizers symbolically interpreted every aspect and moment of the life of Gautama Shakyamuni, explained his theories, narrated the history and development of Buddhism, and reported the lives and thoughts of great monks from every region of the world. It is no exaggeration to say that millions upon millions of pages have been written to express Buddhist faith or to explicate some aspect of Buddhism.

Here are several important examples. The oldest printed book that has been handed down to us is a ninth-century Chinese version of the Diamond Sutra printed from tabular woodcuts. The Buddhist university of Nalanda—attended by 8,500 students and 1,500 teachers every year—also dates to the ninth century. Preserved in its library, once considered the richest in the world, was a copy of every lesson (one hundred lessons were given every day). In 1905, a library dedicated to Buddhist texts in English opened in London, the first such institution in the West for a non-Christian religion. In Tibet monks read the Kanjur, a work of 108 volumes; the Tanjur, with 250 volumes; and numerous treatises of occult science, one of which, the Kuiti, has thirty-five volumes of text and fourteen of commentary. And these were only three of the 648,000 volumes that were once preserved in the monastery of Lhasa, Tibet.

THE LESSER VEHICLE TRADITION

The first school to arise from the controversies of the fourth council was the so-called school of wisdom, the Theravada, also called, by the other schools, with a pejorative connotation, the Lesser Vehicle (Hinayana). It was analytically organized by Shariputra (Sariputra) and constitutes the orthodox image of the oldest Buddhism. Today it exists in Sri Lanka and Indochina.

The teaching of the Theravada school can also be seen as one of the most fascinating moral philosophies of the world, in accordance with reason without imposing irrational and nonscientific dogmas; it is objective and may well be the most tolerant of all the purely spiritual religions. The contemporary school is based on the classical triad: the Buddha as master, Dharma as doctrine, Sangha as way of life. It is both historicist and antinomian: it allows neither a god nor a soul, it believes in the instability of phenomena, in the universal suffering generated by the fact of life, and in reincarnation caused by the desire to live. One can free oneself from the chain of reincarnations by achieving absolute annihilation, nirvana. As the Buddha said, "All matter is illusion. Hold tight to the spirit. Even the spirit is illusion."

What then is reincarnated if the soul does not exist? What is reincarnated is an accumulation of attributes, or characteristics, in continuous evolution that determine character and personality with desires, passions, memories, and preconceptions. The impulses derived from it make us desire life,

Opposite: Brass statue of Ekadashamukha ("eleven-headed") Avalokiteshvara, Ladakh, India.
Below: The large monastery of Polonnaruwa, Sri Lanka.

happiness, possession, honors—and all that is only a reflection of the primary illusion: the self. The glimmer of the moon on a pond is not the moon but only its insubstantial reflection; in the same way the accumulation of actions of a human being, in constant relationship with other such agglomerates, fills the desire for life with negative memories and requires a total purification before annihilation.

Twelve Links of Conditioned Existence, known as the Twelve Nidanas, cause the concatenation of births, configured in the twelve rays of the Wheel of Being: ignorance, aggregation, reflective consciousness, name-form, the five senses, the mind, perception (contact), sensation, desire, attachment, existence, birth-death. Everything begins with nonconsciousness, by the ignorance *(avidya)* that is the cause of the existence of the world, which is illusory and fleeting, and by desire or thirst *(trishna),* thirst for existing, for enjoying, for living the nonexistent.

As expressed by the Lesser Vehicle, a full formulation of the thinking of the Buddha could be summarized as this: We begin with cause and effect; from the cause come passion and action, and from the effect the result. This causes the wheel of life to turn infinitely in an unchanging pattern that can be described as this: Ignorance leads to voluntary activities. Voluntary activities lead to consciousness. From consciousness come the mental and the corporeal. The mental and the corporeal lead to the six senses. From the six senses comes contact. From contact comes sensation. From sensation comes desire. From desire comes attachment. From attachment come actions. Actions cause birth (and rebirth). Every birth leads to old age, death, sorrow, pain, lamentations, desperation. Thus comes into being the great mass of suffering of the world. The first two cycles belong to the past, the next eight to the present, the two last to the future.

There is then the chain of understanding to bring an end to this suffering: the total cessation of ignorance leads to the total cessation of activities; the cessation of activities leads to the cessation of consciousness; the cessation of consciousness leads to the cessation of the mental and the corporeal; the cessation of the mental and the corporeal leads to the suppression of the six spheres of the senses; the cessation of the six spheres of the senses leads to the cessation of contact; the cessation of contact leads to the cessation of sensation; the cessation of sensation leads to the cessation of desire; the cessation of desire leads to the cessation of attachment; the cessation of attachment leads to the cessation of actions; the cessation of actions leads to the cessation of rebirths; the cessation of rebirths leads to the cessation of old age, of death, of sorrow, of pain, lamentations, and desperation. Thus is extinguished the great mass of suffering of the world.

Although strongly mystical at its base, the Lesser Vehicle does not recognize a god, even if it does practice prayer; it seeks to attain an intuitive understanding of the universe through the constant reading of the words of the Buddha. It preaches the value of experience over blind faith and dogma. It recognizes no superiority of caste, gender, or ethnic group, and its sanctuaries are open to all without distinction. In substance, it affirms that "the Buddhist is the person who behaves as the Buddha behaved."

The two major Hinayana sects arose in Cambodia, where the faithful formed the Mahanikaya (Mohanikaya; "great branch"), or traditionalists, and the Thamayut (royal order), or reformists. The Hinayana sects in China are the Lu-Tsung and the Cheng-shih Tsung; in Japan, they are the Kusha, Jojitsu, and Vinaya.

Opposite top and bottom: Two views of Wat Phra Kaeo, the temple in Bangkok, Thailand, built in the late eighteenth century to house the Emerald Buddha.

Right: South terrace of the temple of Borobudur at Java, one of the most important constructions of Mahayana Buddhism. The frieze presents episodes from the Lotus Sutra.

customs, ways of life, and mystical ideals differed from those of India.

First of all, the Mahayana order was open to women. Was this the confirmation of one of the Buddha's prophecies? Against the admission of women to the order, the Buddha had foreseen that their entry, five hundred years after his death, would cause the division of the Dharma. Without doubt, however, the greater spread of Buddhism required a popularization of its original thought. As it became popular, most of all in China and Japan, it was forced to abandon its true intellectual and atheistic nature and take on religious and esoteric characteristics. The ideal was no longer the enlightened disciple *(arhat)* closed in on himself, but rather the saint who had attained the threshold of nirvana but had not entered (had not been annulled), choosing instead to turn back to save those who were still lost in illusion. He thus became a *bodhisattva* ("an enlightenment being," a potential Buddha). For the Great Vehicle this sacrifice of the self was extended to the Buddha, who thus divided into a series of reincarnations presenting his various actions and many teachings.

The Mahayana renewed Buddhism not just in terms of the organization of the monasteries and the religious hierarchy but also on the doctrinal plane and most of all as a result of its three leading thinkers: Nagarjuna, Asanga, and Santideva (or Santiveda).

Nagarjuna (first to second centuries), of Brahman origin, theorized the emptiness of things and was the initiator of relativism in his principal work, the School of the Middle Way (Madhyamika-karika), in which he sought to achieve a reconciliation between the unreal world that is considered real on the basis of empirical truth and the absolute Truth, in the light

The Greater Vehicle's Many Followers

Beginning with the consideration that the doctrine expressed by the old school was incomplete and, in a practical sense, unsatisfactory, a group of learned monks deepened the knowledge of the Hinayana canon, enlarging its concepts. Thus arose the first great formal division, the school of the Greater Vehicle (Mahayana). This school was destined to divide into many rivulets, all of great importance, the results of the enlightened philosophical visions of great masters but also of the practical needs of countries whose uses, of which the real world appears completely unreal.

Asanga (fifth century) was a monist exegete and idealizer of the absolute. According to him, in a universe in which everything is transitory, the only thing that truly has importance is conscience.

Santideva (seventh century) was an authentic mystical poet. According to him, only the ascetic is able to overcome the contingencies of consciousness and the annihilation of nirvana to achieve the understanding that "the condition of being is to be what one is" *(tatha)*. This state can be understood through the "simple notification" or rendered by awareness *(vijnaptimatrata)*.

The Greater Vehicle spread most of all in China and Japan. In those countries, as a result of the freedom sanctioned by the theory of continuous becoming, the basic principle of Buddhism divided into numerous schools. One

Opposite: The monk Zenmui, forerunner of the Japanese Tendai sect, in a twelfth-century Japanese silk painting; Ichijo-yi, Hyogo, Japan.

Below: The monk and chemist Genzi, master of Kukai, founder of the esoteric Shingon sect, in a twelfth-century Japanese painting; Fumon-in, Wakayama, Japan.

Bodhisattvas

" They do not want to earn their own private nirvana. On the contrary, having traveled the deeply sorrowful world of existence and eager to obtain supreme enlightenment, they do not tremble in the face of birth and death. They have set off for the good of the world, out of compassion for the world, to relieve the pains of the world."

Edward Conze,

Buddhism

of the most popular was the Pure Land school, which worshiped one of the five transcendent Buddhas, Amitabha ("Infinite Light, Infinite Splendor, Infinite Time"), also called Amitayusu, Arolika, and Vagisa ("lord of the word"). Popular belief holds that this being, because of his infinite goodness, leads human beings to paradise. In Tibetan depictions he can have one face and two hands but also one face and four hands, three faces and six hands, four faces and eight hands. The Pure Land school spread from China to Japan under the name Jodo and became "the way of salvation through pure faith."

The school of Shin Buddhism was based on a strenuous mystical discipline. Various Sino-Japanese schools were equally progressive in terms of their mystical notions: the Hosso, founded by Dosho; Soran, similar to Hosso, but with a distant Hinayana origin; the Kegon, professed most of all

Opposite: The Lunar Buddha (Gakko Bosatsu) in the Sangatsu-do of the Todaiji temple in Nara, Japan, a work of the eighth century.

Left: View of the Todaiji temple at Nara, erected beginning in 735. In the background is the Daibut-suden, or *kondo* (golden hall), considered one of the most outstanding wooden constructions in the world.

Below: Amida Nyorai in the Kotoku temple at Kamakura, Japan.

The Giant Buddha

In the Todaiji temple (Great Eastern Temple) of Nara, Japan, stands the colossal bronze statue of the Buddha Rushana (Sanskrit: Vairochana), a little over 50 feet high, made on the orders of Emperor Shomu and under the direction of the sculptor Kuninaka-no Kimimaro. It was completed in 753. The statue was partially destroyed in 1180 and 1567 and was reworked in the Edo period in 1692; the base is still the original, in the form of a lotus flower, the petals of which present the worlds that the divinity rules.

Another Japanese Daibutsu (Great Buddha), also 50 feet high, is the Amida Nyorai (Sanskrit: Amitabha Tathagata) in the temple of Kotobu at Kamakura, cast in bronze in 1252, in the style of a great sculptor of the Kaikei period, a student of Kokei.

at Nara in the Todaiji temple, the largest wooden structure in the world, where a fifty-foot-high statue of the Buddha was worshiped; the comparative Tendai school; the liberal, esoteric, and syncretistic Shingon; and the purist and sectarian Nichiren school. When the Kegon, Tendai, and Shingon schools fell into disgrace in Japan, brought down by political events, the common people turned to the Pure Land school, but the military caste, dedicated to its iron code of honor *(bushido),* turned to a sterner form, Zen *(Ch'an* in Chinese). The cultural refinement and depth of expression of Zen are directed at a high form of mystical-intellectual transcendence. In its most active version, that of Rinzai, Zen constitutes the most intellectually enlightened and progressive of the esoteric expressions of Buddhism, being without exterior formalities and popular rituals.

THE TANTRIC VEHICLE

"Hindu Tantrism," which puts the accent on male and female principles and sees the creation of the world as the result of the division of a single divinity, came into being around the fifth century AD, when collections *(tantra)* of rules and magical procedures were assembled in both Brahman and Mahayana India. The influence of Hindu yoga appears in the articulation of certain practices (such as the control of breathing rhythm), while pagan holdovers and elements from the Indus Valley civilization led to attribute great importance to magic words (mantras), with which—if pronounced correctly—one could penetrate the Absolute.

Hindu Tantrism displayed itself in various forms: the *puja*, ritual cult exercise, symbolic of sacrifice and offering; the *asana*, body positions with which the adept awakens the energies of the body or assumes positions reflecting those of the universe, to transcend the material to reach the All; the mantra, a syllable or group of syllables that are spoken or thought in a certain way so as to concentrate cosmic and psychic energies, move vibrating energies, put oneself in tune with them, or create emptiness in the mind; the yantra,

Left: The Bengali monk Atisa (982–1054) and various episodes of his life in a nineteenth-century Tibetan painting. Atisa unified and reformed the Tibetan Buddhist priesthood and founded the strict Kadampa sect, which restored the ancient monastic discipline in accordance with the original Indian sources; Ravi Kuman Foundation, New Delhi, India.

Opposite: A master of the Sakyapa order in a seventeenth-century Tibetan painting; Ravi Kuman Foundation, New Delhi, India.

Shakti divided in her five *kanchuras* (Kali, separator of time; Niyati, producer of dependence; Raga, uniter of separate things; Vidya, knower of separate things; and Kala, cause of action). From this is derived the Prakriti with the three *guna* (qualifications of the material world: purity, action, stasis) and the four ways of thought, origin of the Tatvas, essences or function realities.

This magical-exoteric formula made its first sporadic entries to Tibet during the reign of King Songtsen Gampo (Sron-btsan-sgam-po; reigned 618–694); coming in contact with Buddhism, it developed in an autonomous way, leading to Tibetan Lamaism, also called Tantrayana (Tantra Vehicle), Vajrayana (Diamond-Thunderbolt Vehicle), or Mantrayana (Mantra Vehicle). Thus was born the third major school of Buddhism. The various deified Buddhas and the various

a geometric figure presenting a field of divine or universal energy and in the final analysis thought itself, origin of all, detached from vain mental constructions. In fact, that which most demonstrates the existence in us of a soul is thought.

In this way one repeated the cosmic creation, when Parasmavit (Absolute Unity, including all, the Brahman without qualification) divided into two symbolic divinities: Shiva and Shakti. The first is positive, *prakasha*, the initial male spark of being; the second is negative, *vimarsha*, the female function of being, the mirror of *prakasha*. The union of Shiva and Shakti (symbolized as a sexual union) leads to the Self and the Shakti with its eyes closed, an idealization of the I and the Other, which originates the I and the Shakti with eyes open, which in turn gives origin to the individual I (the Self) and to the Other (the other than the self). From "that" is derived the Maya

Above: The first historical (but according to tradition third) Dalai Lama, Sonam Gyatso (1543–1588), on a nineteenth-century Tibetan *thangka*; Guimet Museum, Paris.

Below: Zanabazar, spreader of Buddhism in Mongolia, in a seventeenth-century painting; Museum of the History of Religion, Ulan Bator, Mongolia.

bodhisattvas were joined to numerous demons of the shamanistic Mongol-Turkish people of the steppe of central Asia. Some of these were incarnations or fragmentary representations of the universal spirit; sometimes they were good or indifferent, at other times they were hostile and fearsome. King Gampo's two Buddhist wives, one Chinese—who caused the conversion of the court to Buddhism—and one Nepalese, were also deified and came to be called Green Tara and White Tara. They are the protective divinities of Tibet.

During the reign of King Trison Deutson (742–797) the "Vehicle" had already conquered the people thanks to the activities of the Indian monk Padmasambhava (also called Guru Rimpoche). By around 1040 it had triumphed throughout Tibet and the nearby territories, thanks to the monk Atisa (Atisha; 982–1054) and to his disciple Milarepa (1040–1143). The autonomous form of Buddhism that came into being considered possible control of the elements, levitation, telepathy, teleportation, resistance to intense cold, and other wonders obtained through knowledge of the way and the use of symbolic hand gestures *(mudras),* ritual words *(mantras),* symbolic diagrams *(yantras),* and painted cosmologies *(mandalas).* At the same time, the monks gradually took over temporal power in the country, eventually running the government. The principal figure in this religious hegemony was the great reformer Tsongkhapa (1358–1419), who founded the Yellow Hats (celibate, or "right hand" monks), as opposed to the Red Hats ("left hand" monks who married and practiced an exaltation of intercourse along with the analogous Hindu practices of Tantrism). He seems to have instituted the positions of the Dalai Lama ("Ocean of Wis-

White Tara in the guise of a sixteen-year-old girl with an *utpala* (edible flower) in her left hand; contemporary wall painting in the *chorten* of Thimbu, Bhutan.

dom"), or king priest, and the Panchen Lama, or chief administrator, positions that led the country until the recent Chinese invasion. The sexual element of the Red Hats, based on the theory of the pairing of opposites, led to the concept of Skaktism, according to which every male principle (deified) has a female counterpart, since the universe exists thanks to the existence of positive and negative principles.

ZEN

Zen (in Indian, Dhyana; in Chinese, Ch'an), the true apotheosis of Buddhism, can also be considered a school unto itself, so much does it sometimes move away from traditional and formal canons of religion understood as a constant repetition of practices and formulas. For Zen, a sacred image used in prayer or contemplation is a useful object, not unlike the kindling tossed into a stove, since the aim of Zen is the overcoming of all worldly formalism. Even the highest culture and the achievement of enlightenment—*satori*—are only means, mere vehicles: reality is always somewhere farther.

It is said that a king once approached the Buddha and, handing him a flower, asked him to explain the law. The Buddha lifted the flower, looked at it a long time in silence, and smiled. After a while, one of his disciples, Mahakashyapa ("Great Kashyapa"), also smiled: he had "understood." Thus was born Zen, which aside from the canonical texts of Buddhism is also based on the great Chinese philosophers of the fifth to first centuries BC, such as Lao-tse and Zhuang Zhou. Developed in China by such thinkers as Huineng (Wei Lang), it took hold most firmly in Japan, where it was introduced around 520 by the Indian philosopher Bodhidharma Daruma. It is said that when Bodhidharma first met the emperor of Japan, and the emperor asked him to explain the principles of Zen, he responded, "The first principle of Zen is vast emptiness." "But then who is standing in front of me?" asked the emperor. "I have no idea" was the response.

Zen attempts to make a sudden leap from thought to an awareness of reality. Such moments are achieved by breaking through the illusory world by way of meditation or nonrational thinking. A good example is the use of koans, short sayings or stories from Zen masters used to induce spiritual intuition.

Examples of koans: "What is the sound of two hands striking one against the other?" asked

the great Zen master Hakuin (1686–1769), who divided koans into five classes: *hosshin* koans to begin the journey; *kikan* koans for initial knowledge; *gonsen* koans to emphasize the importance of words; *nanto* koans, those that are "difficult to penetrate"; and *goi* koans, for understanding the five orders of interdependence of the self. All of this has the scope of achieving *satori*, spiritual enlightenment, detachment from the vacuity of a world that appears real but is instead only illusion. The state of satori cannot be described.

The teachings of Zen had an important effect on ethical behavior (as in the *bushido* of the Japanese samurai) and on the arts, to which it offered the concept of *sunya* (emptiness, absence of all material) and *sunyata* (openness, the transcendence of the world of preconceived ideas). An expression of these concepts can be seen in graphic works, such as paintings, in which one area, usually the lower right corner, is "occupied" by emptiness.

Also emblematic of these teachings are ikebana,

Opposite: Detail of the *Tenju Koku Mandara* (Mandala of Celestial Longevity), embroidery from 622; Chuguji Museum, Ikaruga, Japan.

Above: Silver Pavilion in the Ginkakuji (or Jisho-ji) Zen temple in the Sakyuo-ku section of Kyoto. The original design called for covering the pavilion in silver tiles, hence its name.

Below: Jion Daishi (Ts'enngen), precursor of the Hosso sect, in an eleventh-century painting; Yakushi-ji, Nara, Japan.

Mokurai, clapping his hands. Then he asked, "And what is the sound of one hand clapping?" A student asked the master, "If I have nothing in my mind, what should I do?" "Throw it out," responded the master. "But if I have nothing, how can I throw it out?" "Then keep it!" A master holding nothing in his hand asked his students, "Do you see the spade I am holding in my hand?" "Of course not, you have nothing in your hand." "Good, then take this spade and go dig with it!" A master asked his students, "If I *say* that a goose is shut in a bottle, how would you free it?" and after a series of mistaken answers, "You *say*, 'there, it's free,' and it's free." And finally, "If there is no god, where is god?" To which the response is "Everything is god." The koan system was structured by

the style of flower arrangement; bonsai, the cultivation of dwarf trees; the Japanese tea ceremony; and the rock-and-sand gardens of Japanese temples. In Buddhism, religious scriptures, doctrines, or philosophical systems are merely *ideas* of the truth in the same way that words are not facts but only what is said about the facts. Zen is a vigorous attempt to come into direct contact with the truth itself, without permitting theories or symbols to interfere between the person who hears and the thing that is heard. In a certain sense Zen means living life instead of living a rumor about life; it will admit no secondhand wisdom, no descriptions of experiences, preconceptions, or suppositions. Secondhand wisdom can be useful when it serves to indicate the way, but it is dangerous to mistake it for the way itself or even for the means of travel. The truth can be described in many ways, some of them so subtle that they can themselves be mistaken for the truth; for this reason Zen is iconoclastic and tends to brush aside all purely intellectual images of reality, believing that reality can be known only through personal experience. Thus what others have said becomes valid and is yours only when you yourself hear it, without the existence of any "others" that have said it or a "you" that hears it.

A pedantic man who had studied the history of Zen said to Master Shinkan: "I have long studied the thought of Tendai, but there is one thing I cannot accept: Tendai holds that even the grass and trees can achieve enlightenment. This seems worthy of criticism to me." To which Shinkan responded, "What difference does it make whether the grass and the trees can or cannot achieve enlightenment? What is important is how you can yourself achieve enlightenment. Have you ever asked yourself that?"

The Japanese monk Baozhi opens his skin to reveal the features of Kannon (Japanese name of the Avalokitsehvara Buddha) with eleven faces; wood statue from the Heian period, eleventh century, Saihoji monastery, Kyoto.

BUDDHIST ART IN INDIA

One day the favorite disciple, Ananda, said to the Buddha, "Half of the holy life is friendship, association, and intimacy with the beautiful." To which the Enlightened One responded, "Say not so! It is the whole of the holy life, not half." Indeed, the art brought into being by the Buddhist religion ranks among the most complete, complex, and rich of all the art created by humanity. King Bimbisara (ca. 544–493 BC)—credited with the early spread of Buddhism—founded the great capital Rajagriha. Its thirty miles of walls enclosed the first stone constructions in India. His son Ajatashatru (ca. 493–462 BC), participating in the great cultural and artistic movement generated by the new religion, supported the arts of Bihar. During the Mauryan period (322–185 BC), after the fall of Persepolis, the Greek fashions of Alexander the Great reached India, along with the related concept of art made to serve power, both temporal and religious. Two great rulers, Chandragupta (reigned 323–300 BC) and Ashoka (reigned 274–232 BC), adopted the so-called Indo-Greek column and favored the spread of a Buddhist-style art, translating typically wooden architectural structures into similar structures in stone. Most of all, there was the importance of the most typical Buddhist monument, the stupa, as we will see farther on. The Sunga dynasty (185–72 BC) saw important developments in the monastery *(vihara),* which was given a uniform layout with a central courtyard onto which face the cells of the monks and a larger courtyard for the performance of rites and for public ceremonies, preceded by a hall with statues and frescoes. This typical layout was adopted in other countries. The types of stupa were also enlarged and multiplied, and throughout the Buddhist world great temples were carved out of rock *(caitya)* in which wall painting began to take the place of the bas-reliefs that had been typical of earlier periods.

The period between the first and fifth centuries AD saw a particular flowering in the art of Gandhara, the historic region that is located in today's Pakistan in which Greco-Roman and Indian styles blended.

Adorers of the Buddha, fresco from Cave 24, one of the rock *vihara* dating to the fourth century in the Bamiyan Valley, Afghanistan.

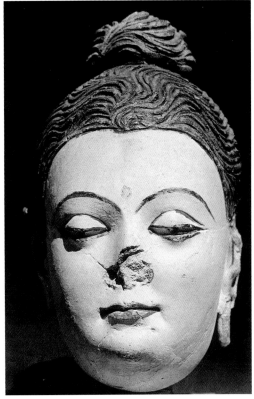

The positions *(asana)* and gestures *(mudra)* of the Buddha were codified on the basis of the attitudes assumed by Roman emperors, while the clothing of the Enlightened One came to imitate the ancient Greek himation. These iconographic motifs spread from the capital of the Kushan rulers (Mathura art) and the Gandhara valley along the Silk Route all the way to China and Japan. At the same time, their rapid spread into southern India resulted in Amaravati art (first to fourth century) and that of the Gupta period (fourth to fifth century). From India, the Greco-Roman-Indian styles were transmitted to Ceylon, Java, and Thailand, but in those places Buddhism took hold more strongly among the people than among the rulers and thus shows up far less in large-scale architecture. Indochina, however—Khmer, Champa, and Sukhothai art—saw the most astonishing examples of large-scale symbolic architecture.

This period saw the formation of many schools and centers of Buddhist art along with the mixing of the various forms of art, much as the religious trends mixed: Buddhism, Jainism, Hinduism, and then Islam.

By the end of the Middle Ages, Buddhist art had degenerated into repetitions and mannerisms of little importance and had lost its central role in Indian art.

Opposite: Preaching Buddha, with hands in the *dharmachakra-mudra*, the gesture of setting in motion the wheel of the law, Gupta period sandstone sculpture, ca. 475; Sarnath.

Above left: Head of the Buddha, Gandharan art, fourth century.

Above right: Head of the Buddha, from the tumulus of Faias Tepe, Sogdian art of the first to second centuries; Uzbekistan Museum, Tashkent.

BUDDHIST ART IN THE FAR EAST

The proliferation of sects and the exposition of their theories, the multiplication of divinities, and the demand for sites of worship had a strong influence on Buddhist art. This influence is most apparent in the countries of the Far East. Various philosophies and rules of life have influenced the positions taken with regard to the tangible expressions of aesthetic taste, most of all in China and Japan. So it is that Buddhism may appear unitary in terms of the Dharma but differs, sometimes considerably, from country to country in terms of its formal appearance.

One of the earliest Buddhist monuments in China is the stone relief of Lianyungang, dated to AD 65, but Buddhist art took hold there between the first and third century, during the Han dynasty and the period of the Three Kingdoms (220–280), during which sculpture, in particular, underwent important development. During the periods of the Three Kingdoms and the Six Dynasties (304–589) the Indian stupa went through a transformation. In Tibet it became a kind of composite tower with complex cosmological symbolism, while in China—

reflecting earlier watchtowers—it became a pagoda with a central layout with from five to fifteen floors emphasized by curving roofs.

The largest Buddhist complex is the cave shrines of Yungang, carved out between 460 and 525, one of the most impressive religious monuments of all humanity. More than fifty caves contain 51,000 statues, one of which is 70 feet high, and several square miles of wall paintings. Thanks to the open-minded views of the Turkic peoples who ruled these areas of China, signs of the art of Ceylon and Gupta are also to be found.

Another colossal complex is the so-called Thousand Buddhas Cave at Qianfodong near Nanjing (Liang period, 502–557). Other large-scale rock works were made in China during the Sui dynasty (581–618), when the figure of the Buddha acquired a characteristic stately nobility.

Under the Tang (618–907) and Song (960–1279) dynasties, the monasteries became powerful fortresses with large square towers; sculpture became more sensitive, painting more rarefied and spiritual, and various learned arts, such as calligraphy, rose to the fore. Notable is the Longmen cave complex (1,352 caves, 97,305 statues, 39 pagodas), the

Left: The Paradise of the West, dominion of the Amitabha, the Buddha of "infinite splendor"; detail of a fresco in Cave 217 of the cave complex at Mogao, Dunhuang, a caravan center in Gansu, China, along the Silk Route; Tang dynasty (628–907).

Opposite: Corner of Cave 9 at Yungang, Datong, Shanxi province; Northern Wei period (386–534). The style of classical decoration arrived in China along the Silk Route.

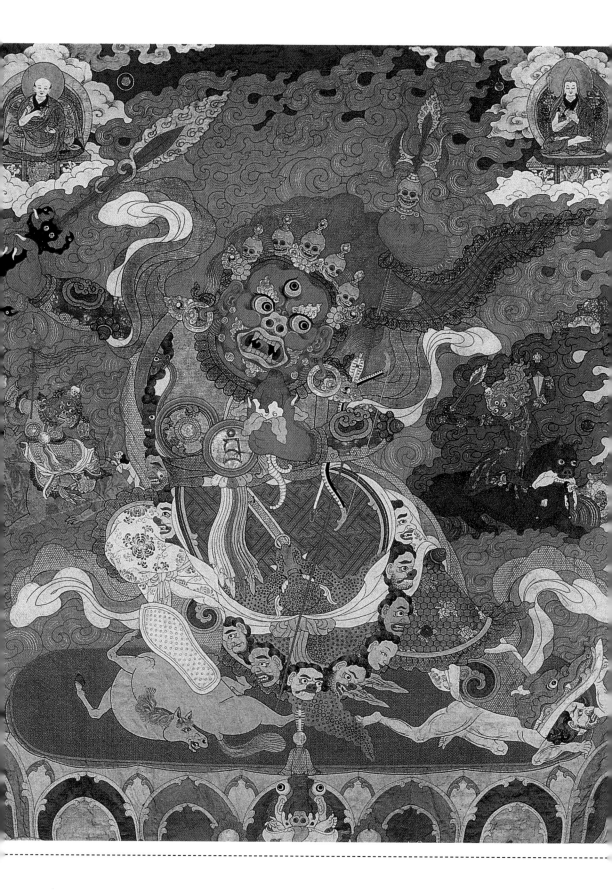

Giant Buddha of Chengdu (232 feet), that of Baod-inghsan (with 1,007 arms), and the 45,000 square feet of mural paintings at Mogao. The Yuan Mongol dynasty (1276–1368) is notable for the barbaric majestic of its wooden statues, while the Ming (1368–1644) reveals the extreme refinement and decadence of an extravagant art destined to decline even further under the Qing (1644–1911).

Buddhism had considerable influence on Japanese art, with results that are unique to Japan. Each of the great historical epochs saw intense cultural and artisan activity, but various masterpieces stand out on their own, such as the most ancient intact temple in the Far East, the Horyuji of Nara (AD 607)—it is also the largest made entirely of wood—

and the colossal bronze statues of Buddha at Nara (749) and at Kamakura (1252), about 60 feet high. Japan also saw the completely autonomous development of art related to Zen, with its taste for the emblematic and its attraction to spaces and lines in a sort of improvisation of gesture that has had an enormous impact on much of contemporary Western art, in particular abstract art.

Opposite: Beg-tse, the "Red Protector," nineteenth-century Mongolian painting; Palace of Bogd Khan, Ulan Bator, Mongolia. Below left: Gilt-bronze *mahasiddha* (great magician), eighteenth-century Mongolian art, from the monastery of Chijin-lama; Museum of the History of Religion, Ulan Bator, Mongolia. Below right: Gilt-bronze *Syamatara* (Green Tara), eighteenth-century Mongolian art; Palace of Bogd Khan, Ulan Bator, Mongolia.

Images of Buddhism: The Stupa

Following the death of the Buddha his followers worshiped three types of "relics" *(caitya)* that could recall the venerable figure of the Enlightened One: his corporeal remains, the sites associated with him, and the objects that had belonged to him or were associated with him. Relics and objects were usually located in what is perhaps the most representative structure of Buddhist religion, the stupa (Tibetan *chorten*): a sort of mound originally made to hold only the relics of the Buddha but later also built to hold the relics of revered teachers or auspicious objects related to various symbolic meanings. The architectural form of the stupa was developed during the first centuries of Buddhism on the basis of earlier sepulchral mounds of saints, whose bodies were placed directly on the ground in a yoga position and then covered with earth. This mound was crowned by a *lingam*, a symbol of the creative power of Shiva and a means of connecting the earthly world with the divine. Among the oldest Buddhist monuments of this genre is that of Sanchi, India, erected by King Ashoka in the middle of the third century BC. It has a body with a brick dome, representing water, atop which stands a square arch, the *harmika*, which contains the offerings of the faithful and represents the earth. Above this, steps symbolic of fire lead to a spire topped

Opposite: The great stupa of Sanchi, India. Sanchi was an important Buddhist center beginning in the third century BC when the emperor Ashoka had a stupa built of brick. One hundred years later it was covered by a hemispherical stone stupa surrounded by a balustrade *(vedika)* that reveals the application of stone to a structure formerly made of wood. In the first century BC (Shunga period) four portals *(torana)* were added facing the four cardinal points, with reliefs of great symbolic intensity. A high terrace *(medhi)* provided a pathway for processions *(pradakshina patha)*. Above the terrace a *harmika* served as the deposit for ex-votos. The entire structure was topped by three circular disks *(chattra)* as "parasols of honor."

Right: Chinese pagoda with seven floors, today known as the Tower of the Bell, 1384; Xian, Shanxi, China.

by three symbolic umbrellas, the *chattra*, symbolic of the wind (in that time and place the umbrella or parasol was symbolic of royalty). All of this is then topped by the "twin symbol" that unites the sun and moon. This structure was enclosed by a high balustrade with openings *(torana)* and richly decorated with bas-reliefs.

Both Ashoka, in the third century BC, and King Kaniska, in the first century AD, were great builders of stupa shrines. These first monuments inspired both the Indian *shikhara* (in which the walls of the base were richly decorated with bas-reliefs) and the Chinese pagoda. The pagoda was also based on ancient Chinese watchtowers and from the earliest examples (such as the Wild Goose Pagoda near Xian, from AD 701) had the form of a tall building with a central layout and a succession of seven to fifteen roofs.

To Buddhists the entire stupa is symbolic of the route to enlightenment, from worldly miseries to the sublime state of the divine spirit.

Individual stupas or groups of them—usually

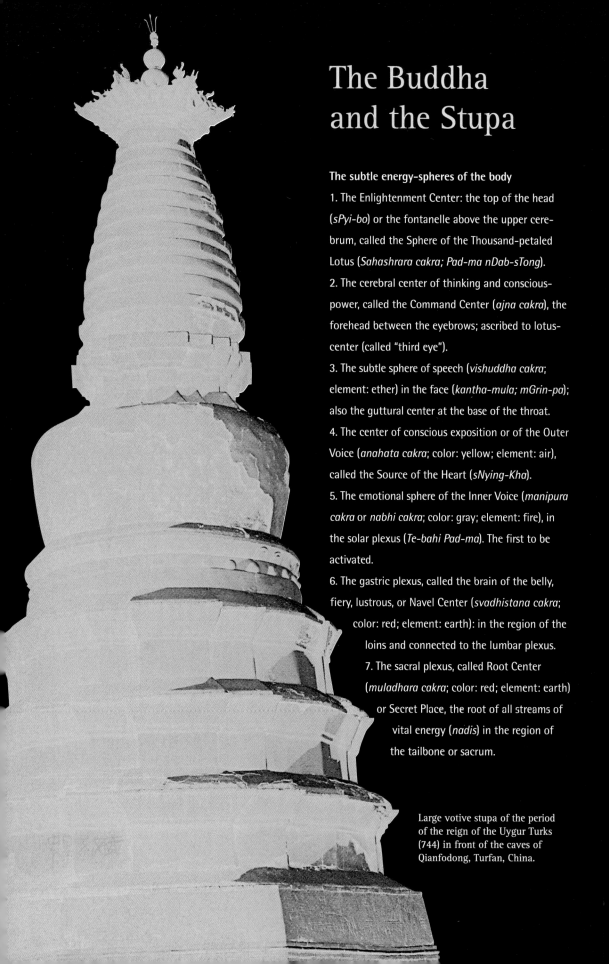

The Buddha and the Stupa

The subtle energy-spheres of the body

1. The Enlightenment Center: the top of the head (*sPyi-bo*) or the fontanelle above the upper cerebrum, called the Sphere of the Thousand-petaled Lotus (*Sahashrara cakra; Pad-ma nDab-sTong*).

2. The cerebral center of thinking and conscious-power, called the Command Center (*ajna cakra*), the forehead between the eyebrows; ascribed to lotus-center (called "third eye").

3. The subtle sphere of speech (*vishuddha cakra*; element: ether) in the face (*kantha-mula; mGrin-pa*); also the guttural center at the base of the throat.

4. The center of conscious exposition or of the Outer Voice (*anahata cakra*; color: yellow; element: air), called the Source of the Heart (*sNying-Kha*).

5. The emotional sphere of the Inner Voice (*manipura cakra* or *nabhi cakra*; color: gray; element: fire), in the solar plexus (*Te-bahi Pad-ma*). The first to be activated.

6. The gastric plexus, called the brain of the belly, fiery, lustrous, or Navel Center (*svadhistana cakra*; color: red; element: earth): in the region of the loins and connected to the lumbar plexus.

7. The sacral plexus, called Root Center (*muladhara cakra*; color: red; element: earth) or Secret Place, the root of all streams of vital energy (*nadis*) in the region of the tailbone or sacrum.

Large votive stupa of the period of the reign of the Uygur Turks (744) in front of the caves of Qianfodong, Turfan, China.

Analogy with the symbolism of the stupa

1. The principle of Highest Enlightenment (*bindu; Thig-le*) or Tongue of Flame (*nada; Thig-le*): to be located above the double symbol crowning the *chorten*.

2. The double symbol (*surya candra; Nyi-Zla*) of the Sun and Rising Moon (*Zla-Tshes*), an emblem of the meaning of the Twin-unity of Absolute Truth (of the spiritual sphere) and Relative Truth (of the worldly sphere).

3. Thirteen stylized parasols (*chattra; gDugs*), symbols of royalty giving protection from all forces of evil; and thirteen Wheels of the Law. These are symbols of the thirteen Steps of Enlightenment, or the first ten Steps of Enlightenment (*dasha-bhumi; Byang-chub*).

4. The three higher levels of supraconsciousness (*avenika-smritypushthana; Dran-pa Nye-bar bZhang-pa*), expressed by the three elements of the "head piece."

5. The dome (or pot), corresponding to the primeval mound (stupa), as Receptacle of Relics or Offerings (*dhatu-garbha; mChod-rten*); the ancient Indian stupas were also called eggs (*anda*).

6. The steps that symbolize the ascent of matter to spirituality, from the darkness of egoism to the light of awareness (*nara loka Mi-Yul*); the treasure of the book: *gTerma*.

7. The throne, or base (*parisanda; Bang-rim*), is square and with four steps, its sides facing the four directions; it is symbolic of the world.

The subtle energy-spheres of the body

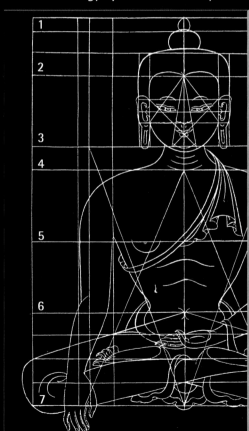

The analogy with the symbolism of the stupa

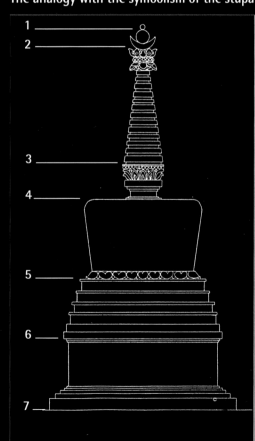

bell-shaped—were erected on sacred sites and along pilgrimage routes. In the Tibetan codification there were usually eight (the eight great *mahacaitya*), symbolic of the eight most important moments of the Buddha: the first *(kutam chorten)* is dedicated to his birth; the second *(labab chorten)* to his

ascent to the heaven of the gods; the third *(namgyal chorten)* symbolizes the power (primarily that of the goddess Namgyalma) to prolong life; the fourth *(chothul chorten)* refers to the faculties that permitted the Buddha to struggle against the forces of evil when they sought to prevent him from

reaching enlightenment; the fifth *(dututul chorten)* symbolizes his victory over those forces; the sixth *(jangchub chorten)* is emblematic of the final victory, of purity, of ultimate liberation; the seventh *(papung chorten)* is dedicated to the sermon of the Buddha on the three paths that lead to the liberation of the spirit; and the eighth *(myangda chorten)* is dedicated to the moment in which the Buddha achieved nirvana. The symbolism goes well beyond this simple level, since the shape of the structure is related to the body of the

Buddha, and as the perfect proportions of the golden section were used in the statuary of the first centuries (particularly in that of Gandhara) the various parts of the stupa are equated with the six parts of the body of the Enlightened One (center of enlightenment or brain; cerebral center or face; guttural center or neck; center of fire or cardiac plexus; center of water or solar plexus; center of earth or sacral plexus); examining the stupa from top to bottom reveals analogies: the double symbol that is the terminal crown, the stylized parasols, the thirteen steps, the dome, and the base.

Opposite top: The stupa of Gaochang (Chinese Turkestan) from the Tang period (628–906). The shape of the stupa is emblematic of the Sermon at Benares (Varanasi), with the Buddha at the center and four students indicating the four corners.

Opposite bottom: Small votive stupas from the period of the reign of the Uygur Turks, (744), in front of the caves of Qianfodong, Turfan, China.

Sculpture in the shape of a stupa, eighteenth-century Mongolian art; Fine Arts Museum, Ulan Bator, Mongolia.

Images of Buddhism: The Mandala

The term *mandala* is from the Sanskrit *mandel*, "circle, round," a term used widely throughout central Asia. In Mongolia there are the cities of Mandel-Gobi and Mandel-Bulag; the city of Mandel in Afghanistan was an enemy of Herat; the southeast coast of India is called the Coromandel Coast, and the name is applied to a kind of precious Indian lacquers.

In iconography a mandala is a two-dimensional diagram of a sacred or spiritual realm. At the center is the *kutagara*, the "sanctuary of the sovereign," containing the statue of the god to whom the mandala is dedicated ("the sovereign of the mandala": *mandalesha*); if this happens to be one of the five transcendent Buddhas, the other four are located around him. The sanctuary

Below: The design of a large mandala seen frontally and, opposite, the same mandala created in colored sand by monks for a Tantric rite in the Sakya at Thimbu in Bhutan. It takes the Tibetan monks several months to prepare a sand mandala, and the rite usually lasts only a few days, after which the work is destroyed, emphasizing a fundamental teaching of Buddhism on the "impermanence of all composite things."

is surrounded by one or more concentric, circular, or square galleries, often divided into cells for numerous divinities to inhabit. This whole is enclosed within a wall with four doors open to the four cardinal points and protected by ferocious divinities, and it is often surrounded by a large circle, ideally presenting a sphere since the nadir and the zenith should ideally be added to the four cardinal points. This circle is composed of three emblematic strips: the mountain of fire, the belt of diamonds, and the belt of lotus petals. Some mandalas include more walls or contain five or six small mandalas arranged within a common wall. Not all mandalas present the figures of divinities; some give instead their names or syllables emblematic of their names. There are usually thirty-seven sovereigns of mandalas, giving rise to thirty-seven principal types of presentation.

At an early time—although they are still made today—mandalas were made of colored sand and were swept away at the completion of the ceremony they had been made for. They were used for

The Mandala

"The magic circles of a mandala mark off, in a profane setting, magical areas in which all the forces of the universe can be brought into play, appeased, or controlled by the celebrant through the recitation of magic formulas."
Jean Filliozat, *Le Bouddhisme*

The Mandala

Mandala is from the term *mandel*, "circle"; in
Tibetan it is *dKyl-'khor*. Symbolic representations
of a mystic, cosmological character—and thus
typical of Tibetan Buddhism—they are circular
depictions of the universe. They can also be
looked upon as the layout of a temple, with
various divinities (Tathagata, bodhisattvas,
and others) at the cardinal points. These
cardinal points are usually in a characteristic color: west is red, south is
yellow, east is blue, north is green.
These colors extend from side to
side, thus dividing the mandala in
four parts. The east (from which
the enumeration of the divinities
always begins) is below, the west
above, the south to the right,
and the north to the left. The
corners (*kona*) are located at the
direction points even when the
mandala is round. There one finds
the Direction Guardians (*dikpala*):

toward the zenith and one toward the nadir, on the same vertical line as the divinity of the mandala. There are thirty-six different types of mandala, aside from the "great mandala" (*mahamandala*), composed of five or six small mandalas surrounded by a wall. Instead of pictorial images some mandalas contain symbols of the divinities or evoke them with "seed" letters (*bija*). A mandala with a pictorial representation is called a *kaya-mandala* ("body mandala"); a mandala with a symbol is a *citta-mandala* ("thought mandala"); a mandala with a "seed" letter is an *an-mandala* ("word mandala").

the southeast is Agneya, the southwest is Nairrtya, the northwest is Vayavya, and the northeast is Aisanya. At the center is the sanctuary (*kutagara*) enclosing the *mandalesha*, the sovereign or meditation divinity or the divinity of the wheel (*cakresha*). Its place can also be taken by a lotus flower with the divinity at the center and the acolytes in the petals (the nearest are usually in the eight petals surrounding the center). The sanctuary is encircled by one or more concentric galleries (*pattika*), sometimes divided in houses (*kosthaka*). The whole is closed by a square wall (*prakara*) with four portals (*torana*), one for each cardinal point. In some cases Hindu divinities or personified abstractions or even the eight cemeteries (*smasana*) are located outside this wall. Finally the whole is contained within a protective circle (*raksacakra*), an image of the Wheel (*cakra*), although ideally it corresponds more closely to a sphere or a top, with eight rays (*ara*) toward the cardinal and side points plus one ray

Opposite: Sambara mandala, sixteenth-century Tibetan art; Guimet Museum, Paris.

Above: Chinese mandala with the symbol of *vishvavajra*, carved in the seventh century; Peking Gate of the Great Wall.

Below: Contemporary interpretation of the symbolism of the mandala; the five principal religions symbolized by *mantram* converge at the center in the symbol of mysticism.

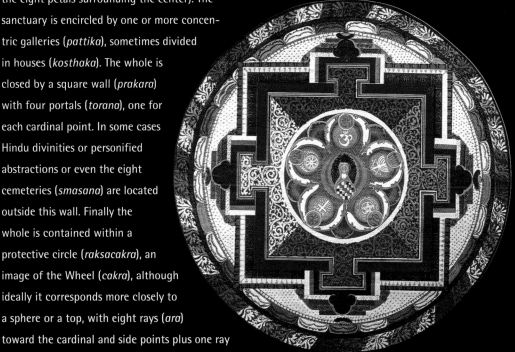

purposes of meditation and for initiation ceremonies. During the initiation, the neophyte monk,
led by his master, traced the diagram with his eyes,
studying the divinities and their positions, looking
into the different areas and, arriving at the heart
of the labyrinth, mentally joining with the value-
symbol of the sovereign of the mandala. When the
mandala is used for mediation, its "sites" are also
visited with the eyes, penetrating its transcendent and esoteric meanings. A similar but more carefully planned
event takes place with a
painted mandala. These
also follow a basic layout:
at the center of a square is
the *kutagara*, the sanctuary of the sovereign. When the
mandala is made with painted sand, the
central square is divided by two diagonals into
four parts with special colors: the lower part, the
east, an auspicious region, is blue; to the left is the

Above: Some of the 72 perforated stupas that compose
the "Sphere of the Not-
Form." These stupas represent the 72 basic elements,
the "dharmas," that form
together variously to gener-
ate the five *skandhas*
("aggregates") of which
every human body is com-
posed; Borobudur, Java.

Below: Drawing of the
Borobudur complex.

Opposite: Detail of the
band of bas-reliefs that
relates the Kamadhatu
("The Sphere of Desire").
In this section, with its
scenes of daily life, the
Buddha takes human form.

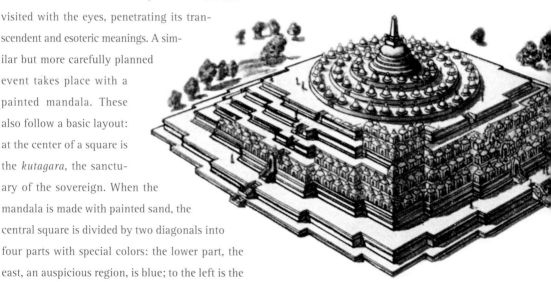

south, colored yellow; above is the west, red; to the right is the north, green. Aside from divinities, the seven treasures of the universal sovereign are often presented (the wheel of the law, the jewel of the desires, the virtuous queen, the wise minister, the elephant, the race horse, the victorious general) or the eight auspicious signs (the parasol, the symbol of royalty; two golden fish; the vase of jewels; the lotus flower; the conch shell; the endless knot; the round flag; the wheel).

Aside from the mandalas made of colored sand and ones that were painted, there are also mandalas composed of vast architectural complexes, such as Borobudur of Java (ninth century), the Kumbum stupa of Gyantse in southern Tibet (1427), and the Tamshing Bumthang of Bhutan (ca. 1433). Observation of these constructions leads to the conclusion that the diagram of the mandala probably originated in the stupa shrines containing relics of the Buddha, for these were often surrounded by smaller-size votive structures. In these large buildings (a typical example is Borobudur), the path for meditation and worship is actually followed physically, not mentally.

Borobudur

This monumental stone structure located in the center of Java was built by the Sailendra dynasty in the early ninth century AD. Spread across a round hill, the structure is composed of nine receding terraces rising from a broad base about 440 feet on a side. The three top terraces are bordered by small, bell-shaped stupas, 72 in all, each containing an image of the Buddha within a perforated cover. Sculpted panels—about 1,300 in all—illustrate scenes from the life of the Buddha, with sharp details and highly realistic modeling. The complex is the architectural presentation of a mandala interweaving cosmological and dynastic symbols.

TIBET: LAND OF IMAGES AND CIRCLES

Tibetan iconography may well be the most meaningful, mysterious, evocative, and picturesque of all the vast and complex Buddhist pantheon. A primary reason for this is that Tibetan art involves the precise illustration of religious notions and philosophical concepts: even the smallest details must correspond to precise rules.

Gestures, sizes, colors, and attitudes have meaning and are reproduced with scrupulous fidelity meant to transmit the power of the divinity-symbol. Every figure-concept is presented both as "wisdom" *(prajna)*, with a female appearance, and as "means" *(upaya)*, with a male appearance.

The relative sizes of the figures are based on a canonical hierarchy. When a group of divinities is presented, the size of each in relation to the others is the result of strict rules. There are also two broad typological categories: serene figures and those that are fierce.

Also important are presentations of the corporeal signs of the Buddha thanks to which he can be recognized. There are thirty-two major auspicious attributes *(lakshanas)* and eighty minor *(anuvyanjanas)*. The omnipotence and omnipresence of the god are symbolized by multiplying the number of faces, hands, or feet; by means of

Left: Fourteenth-century Tibetan *thangka* depicting an *arhat* with assistants. The faces, not typically Tibetan, are based on Chinese paintings of the Southern Song or Yuan dynasties. The right hand holds a staff composed of bamboo canes tied with cords; the left forms the gesture of teaching.

Opposite top: Vajrabhairava in Yab-Yum, Central Tibet, seventeenth century. This protective divinity is presented in physical union with a *prajna*. While he has many arms and heads, she has only one head and two arms. Both are in belligerent attitudes. Of his nine heads, only that at the top, Manjushri, is peaceful. Although of Indian origin, this divinity was invoked during new year's festivals by both the Sakyapa and the Nyingmapas sects since it was a fusion of shamanistic and Buddhist rituals.

Opposite bottom: Buddha Maitreya, one of the incarnations of the future Buddha.

the bell *(ghanta)* and the "diamond thunderbolt" *(vajra)*; they are present in all the esoteric rites except for those from certain cultural areas. There is also the three-bladed ritual dagger called the *phur-bu*.

These objects often appear in the hands of divinities. The *vajra* are related in particular to the sixteen Vajra-bodhisattvas associated, in groups of four, to the peripheral Jinas; the names of another one hundred twenty-four minor divinities begin with "Vajra," and to these can be added others that are better known by other names.

gestures; by means of the objects he holds; by means of the pedestal on which the figures stand; by means of clouds and aureoles; by means of the animals or anthropomorphic beings that accompany them; by means of the mode of transportation, whether by animal or vehicle.

The gods are distinguished by their attitudes—standing, seated, lying down, kneeling, flying—and by their attributes, most of all special objects or animals. Arms and hands range from two to ten to thirty-four or even more. Other characteristics that distinguish the various divinities (or deifications) are hairstyle and, most of all, color. A complete repertory of the divinities lists nearly nine hundred and fifty, from A to Z (more correctly from Acala, "the immobile," a protector of the mandala, with a ferocious appearance, in the colors black and blue and rarely white, to Yogini, various witches and fates that are female Tantric deities).

The two main objects in the magical-religious rituals of Tantric Buddhism are

The term *diamond thunderbolt (vajra)* gives a poor notion of the concept meant by the Sanskrit name, which includes the idea of light, of purifying warmth, of incorruptibleness, of the male member. The Vajryana school (Diamond Vehicle) attaches various esoteric specifications and mysterious rites to each of these values. The vajra has a specular appearance, being composed of the union of two open globular shapes, each of which is composed of a central bar surrounded by from four to eight spokes. There is also an attribute composed of two vajra arranged to form a cross. This is the so-called *vishvavajira*, the universal thunderbolt or the twelve-pointed vajra, and its four points threaten the four cardinal points. It can have the five colors of the five Tathagatas and is the particular characteristic, among other divinities, of Amoghasiddha.

The bell (*ghanta* or *vajraghanta*: the diamond bell, in Tibetan *dzilbu*) can be simple or elaborate, in which case it bears the face of a divinity *(prajna)* on its handle, while its sides are decorated with eight syllables, often presented amid open lotus petals; the syllables represent the eight secondary divinities assisting the principal; the sides may also bear decorations and auspicious signs. In some instances the handle of a bell may repeat the typology of a vajra. Every bell has a clapper, although by preference the bell is rung by running a wooden pestle along its edge in a circular movement.

When a vajra and *ghanta* are put together (most of all in portraits, the first in the right hand, the second in the left), the vajra represents the means for reaching awakening and the ghanta the wisdom necessary to achieve that enlightenment. According to Tibetan tradition, iron from meteorites is usually added to the metals used in the casting of these objects, and indeed meteorites are numerous in the Tibetan highlands.

Opposite: Tibetan *thangka* depicting Dorjey Drolo in a secret form. This male Tibetan divinity is armed with a *phur-bu* (sacrificial knife) and *rDo-rhe* (lightning) and rides a tiger; eastern Tibet, second half of the eighteenth century.

Above right: Ceremonial tambourine of a red lama; Potala, Lhasa, Tibet.

Above center: Tibetan bronze *phur-bu* from the fifteenth century. This three-bladed knife was designed to defeat demons and overcome the attachment to passions.

Above: Tibetan bronze "Diamond thunderbolt" (*vajra*; *dorje* in Tibetan) from the late eighteenth century; Lhasa, Tibet.

BUDDHISTS TODAY

Although open to other continents by sea and by ocean, Europe was closed to foreign religious ideologies until the eighteenth century. Recognition of the equality of differing value systems was first advanced by the French philosopher and author *Representation*). Schopenhauer foresaw a "radical change in our science and our thinking" as a result of increased awareness of Buddhism. On this route the religion of the Enlightened One also touched, although with a different result, composer Richard Wagner and the philosopher Nietzsche.

Discontent with various aspects of Western

Voltaire, followed by a host of other thinkers during the age of Enlightenment, but only in the nineteenth century did Buddhism begin to find acceptance and followers in the West, and it did so as a result of two trends. One of these was drawn to the positivism inherent in it; the other found appeal in its profound exoticism. Buddhism was also seen as a religion of nihilism, and as such it had considerable influence on the works of the German philosopher Arthur Schopenhauer (*The World as Will and*

Above: Offerings in a temple in Bangkok.

Opposite: The Wat Phra Kaeo of Bangkok. Erected in 1767, in imitation of the late Ayutthaya style, to hold the Emerald Buddha (Phra Kaeo), a statue taken from the king of Laos that then became the palladium of Siam (known as Thailand since 1948). Detail of the northern path, with view of the great lateral stupa.

civilization has often led certain people both to predict its collapse and to look elsewhere for alternatives. One result of this has been an increasing desire to understand other religions, particularly the teaching of the Buddha. Today this desire is particularly strong among young people, and it is unnecessary to list the quite valid reasons for this ideological revolution. We do not know the exact terms of this "renewal" of Buddhism today. We can state that in the Western world the Buddhist centers, in particular those of the Tibetan school, have been increasing, and an increasingly large number of Tibetan monks now live in the West, collecting converts. General numbers can be given for the world's Buddhists (Lesser Vehicle, 35 million; Trantra Vehicle, 3 million; Greater Vehicle, 40 million), but these are absolutely hypothetical numbers, for the establishment of an

accurate count is thwarted by the political disturbances in Tibet, Indochina, and Indonesia, and by the success—although hard to define—of Chinese communism (although China did not have a large number of Buddhists).

In China there is an active Buddhist Association, formerly directed by Zhao Puchu (1907–2000). At Sarnath (Benares), along with the sites where the Buddha preached, there is a statue of Anagarika Dharmapala (1864–1933), the Buddhist activist who in 1891 founded the Maha Bodhi Society, an institution that assists pilgrims in India and restores the sacred sites of Buddhism. In 1992, the Lama Gangchen founded the Lama

Gangchen World Peace Foundation, which publishes *Peace Times*. Its headquarters are in Milan, Italy, and it has branches worldwide. These are only a very few examples that testify to the vitality of Buddhism and the uninterrupted continuity of its word and its law, which are still being brought to every corner or the world and directed at every person, without distinction of class or skin color, as is fitting for a great religion that leads humans from the unknown to the Known along a path of goodwill, peace, and light.

Above: Statue of the king-lama president of Hinayana Buddhism in Bangkok.

Below: Group of young Buddhist monks in Sri Lanka.

Thus Spoke
Aphorisms and Thoughts of the Buddha

From the Digha Nikaya

Earthly life is brief; one dies before a hundred years, and anyone who lives longer lives decrepit. Men torment themselves because of attachment, for there are no lasting goods. But like the man who, on awakening, no longer sees the phantasms of his dreams, he that has defeated attachment lives serenely.

Free yourselves absolutely from evil and then free yourselves absolutely from good, like the man who reaches the opposite shore and abandons the raft he used to get there, by then useless.

Everything ends, nothing ends; everything exists, nothing exists.

The wise man moves ahead keeping his senses in check and controlling his faculties, firm in the doctrine, finding joy in rectitude, overcoming attachment, and thus freeing himself from anxiety. Thus he is not contaminated by what he sees and hears, and thus he will not be touched by the corruption of the world.

He who is healthy of mind does not compete with the world, nor does he condemn it. Through meditation he knows that nothing here is lasting except the troubles of living.

Like the king who enjoys seeing himself as the sole ruler amid thousands of men, he who has obtained awareness enjoys thinking of himself as the sole master of his mind amid thousands of men.

When the moment is right friends are pleasing; amusing oneself is pleasing; a good job is pleasing. But far more pleasing is the renouncement of pain at the hour of death.

In this world the condition of a mother is pleasing; the condition of a father is pleasing; the condition of the ascetic is pleasing; the condition of the Brahman is pleasing. Pleasing is virtue that endures into old age; pleasing is faith that puts down firm roots; pleasing is the conquest of knowledge. Most pleasing of all, however, is knowing how to avoid sin.

Since hate never ceases with hate, hate will cease with love; this is a very old rule.

It seems that not everyone here knows that everyone must come to an end; but those who know it immediately stop struggling.

If a man speaks or acts from a bad thought, the result for him is pain, like the wheel that follows the foot of the ox pulling the cart. If a man speaks and acts from a pure thought, the result for him is happiness, like the shadow that never leaves him.

"He mistreated me, he struck me, he defeated me, he stole from me." In those who harbor such thoughts as these, hate will never cease.

He who lives without seeking pleasures, firmly controlling his senses, eating moderately, and remaining faithful and strong will not be defeated by temptation, like a mountain of rock cannot be blown down by the wind.

He who wishes to wear the yellow robe of the monk without being purified of sin, without observing temperance and the truth, sometimes lying, is not worthy of it.

Those who imagine the true in the false and see the false in the true never achieve happiness but follow vain desires.

Just as rain penetrates a house through a poorly constructed roof, passion penetrates the mind that does not know how to reflect.

He who does wrong cries in this world and will cry in the future world. He will cry in both worlds and will suffer, seeing the bad result of his own acts.

He who works good will be happy in this world and in the next, since he who works good is happy when he thinks of the good he has done and even more because he follows the right path.

The unreflective man, even if he knows part of the law by heart and can recite it from memory, is not part of it, like he who counts the cows that belong to another.

He who follows the law even if he does not know it by heart but abandons passion, hate, and foolishness, possesses true knowledge and peace of mind. Without worry for the things of this world, nor for those of the future world, he possesses true serenity.

No longer is there suffering for those who have made the journey and abandoned pain, for those who are freed on every side and have thrown away all fetters. With all their thoughts collected, they dedicate themselves and do not linger in their homes; like swans that have left their lake, they abandon their home and their hearth.

It is hard to understand the route taken by those who have no wealth, who live on frugal food, who have realized emptiness and unconditional freedom, just as it hard to understand the route taken by the birds in the air.

Like a lake without mud is he whose senses have been brought under control, like horses held tight by the reins of the driver; he who is free from pride and from desire, he who performs his duty and is as welcoming as the earth or a threshold. For him there are no new births to come.

He whose thoughts are tranquil, and whose words and acts are tranquil, has obtained freedom by means of awareness and has become a man of peace.

The man who is free of credulity, who knows that which has not been created, who has cut all ties, distanced all temptations, renounced all desires, is the greatest man of all.

In a hovel or in the forest, on the sea or on dry land, anywhere that venerable people live is a place of delight.

After seeing the gray bones thrown away like gourds in the autumn, what pleasure remains to life? Those bones are used to build a fortress that is then covered with skin and blood and in it live old age and death, along with pride and deceit.

As splendid as they are, the chariots of the king . . . will be destroyed. The body too makes its way toward destruction, but the virtue of the good people will never be destroyed.

A man is not old when his hair is gray but is called old if, at a mature age, he has aged to no purpose.

In the highest of the ethereal heavens, in the heaven whose essence is beyond conception, a life of many millions of centuries is lived, but even there everything has an end, everything perishes.

I have revealed the knowledge that destroys the roots of life and death. Nor, after my nirvana, will this knowledge perish with me. It will continue forever in thought and in performance of the right practice and the right thinking.

The good man respects his elders, is not jealous of them; at the proper time he goes in search of teachers and knows how to behave and move in their presence. He listens with respect to words of wisdom.

The good man finds delight in culture, finds joy in knowledge, holds tight to the Dharma, has the right understanding of the science, does not participate in discussions that are irreverent of the doctrine, but guides himself, expressing himself with right and honest words. He abandons hilarity, desire, lamentations, hate, falsity, hypocrisy, greed, vainglory, ire, harshness, the fundamental sins, and infatuation.

At the right time, after ridding himself of all arrogance, the good man goes to teachers. He turns his mind to what is useful, to knowledge, to self-control, to the condition of perfect purity. He puts these in practice.

The good man behaves without arrogance and is firm in his spirit. He excels in thought and action and is constant in calm, in benevolence, in concentration. He will achieve perfection in knowledge and in awareness.

Much unhappiness is derived from malevolence and from foolish offenses committed only to please personal vanity and pride.

If a stupid man does me harm, I will give him the protection of my love in exchange without resentment; the more harm he does me, the more good will go from me to him. The fragrance of good will flow to me and the harmful air of evil will flow increasingly to him.

As the echo belongs to the sound and the shadow to the substance, so unhappiness always falls on he who does bad.

A wicked man who reproaches a virtuous man is like the man who looks up and spits at the sky; the spit does not soil the sky but falls back to soil the wicked man.

The dead are like mature fruits about to fall; once reborn, they are about to die.

Like terra-cotta vases forever in danger of breaking, so the life of a human is always in danger of ending.

Young or old, wise or foolish, all are subject to death. Overcome by death, a father cannot save a child, nor can parents save their own parents.

Peace of mind is obtained with neither pleasure nor regret. On the contrary: following pleasures or tormenting oneself with regret one is overtaken by an even greater sorrow, and the body suffers even more.

No matter how much an ill man laments or cries over his pain, such laments and tears will not save him from death.

He that has broken the arrow of pain and has become serene will obtain peace of mind. He that has been able to overcome and to defeat pain will be free from all pain.

The greatest happiness a mortal human can imagine is the bond of marriage, which joins together two bodies in love. There is yet an even greater happiness: it is the embrace of the Truth. Death separates husband and wife, but death will never have power over the human being joined in marriage to the Truth.

If someone finds fault with me or the Law or the community, seek to discern what is false and to recognize it as false. If someone praises me or the Law or the community, do not take it with joy or exaltation or enjoyment of any kind, for if you are happy or exultant or content it will be an obstacle to you.

In truth, the praise that a common man directs at me is completely insignificant, minimal, and purely moral; and insignificant, minimal, and purely moral is how you should take it.

The Buddhist avoids harming living things, has put away the cane, has put away the sword, is modest and compassionate and lives determined to do good to all living things.

The Buddhist avoids taking what has not been given him, has only what has been given him, lives with a purified soul and knows nothing of theft.

The Buddhist eats one meal only, fasts in the evening, abstains from eating outside the fixed times. He does not attend wicked shows, dancing, singing. He does not wear ornaments or dress his hair or put on garlands, perfumes, salves. He does not have soft or large beds, does not accept gold or money.

The Buddhist neither bears nor sends messages, neither buys nor sells, does not dispute weights, money, or measures. He doest not fall into intrigues, does not deceive, does not cheat. He does not wound or kill, does not imprison, does not associate with brigands, does not pillage, does not perform acts of violence. The day will come in which this world, after a very long time, will be annihilated. When it is annihilated the beings will reach a radiant state. In that state they will be pure spirit, nourished by joy, luminous. They will move through space in their joy, which will endure for a long, long time.

After we have adequately recognized the formation and the dissolution of perceptions, with their taste, their misdeeds, and when we have finally recognized the way to escape them, then we will be unconditionally free.

It might also happen that a religious man, a Brahman, thanks to his ardor, his energy, his dedication, his vigilance, his perfect attention to the spirit, will achieve such a concentration of thinking that he will succeed, even while living in this world, in understanding, as we monks understand, that the world is infinite.

This world is infinite, without limits. For what reason? I, thanks to my ardor, to my energy, to my dedication, my vigilance, to my perfect attention to the spirit, have achieved such a concentration of thinking that, having concentrated my thoughts myself I have seen the world with the awareness that it is infinite. For this I know that the world is infinite, without limits.

There are profound themes, difficult to understand, difficult to see, serene, elevated, inaccessible to reasoning, subtle, understandable only to the wise. Those are what I communicate to you when I see them thanks to my superior knowledge, and for which one might well weave a truthful eulogy in my honor.

From the Small Sutra of the Prince of Hetimandel

Just as none of us is born clothed, none of us is born prepared to support life; but our spirit must clothe itself in understanding for the imperfections of life, for its natural events, for its adversities and sorrows.

There are three roots of life: that which is inside ourselves, that which is outside ourselves, that which is above us. Respect for the three ways, fulfillment of one's duties to the three ways, devotion to the beauty of these three roots permits us to make the tree of our life flourish.

From the Brahmajalasuttam Pathamam

There are religious people who believe in eternity, proclaim that the self and the world are eternal, and this in four forms. This is the experience of people who do not know, who do not see; this is the fervor and the contortion of people in prey to the thirst for being.

There are religious people who like eels slip away from any question put to them; they speak vaguely and do so under four forms. This is the experience of people who do not know, who do not see; this is the fervor and the contortion of people in prey to the thirst for being.

There are religious people who concern themselves with the first ages, speculate on the first ages, enunciate dogmas based on the first ages, and propose these dogmas in different ways and in eighteen chapters. This is the experience of people who do not know, who do not see; this is the fervor and the contortion of people in prey to the thirst for being.

There are religious people who affirm the existence of a Self that is conscious after the destruction of the body, they proclaim the survival of the spirit after the destruction of the body, and do so in sixteen chapters. This is the experience of people who do not know, who do not see; this is the fervor and the contortion of people in prey to the thirst for being.

There are religious people who affirm the existence of a Self that is conscious after the destruction of the body, and do so in eight forms. This is the experience of people who do not know, who do not see; this is the fervor and the contortion of people in prey to the thirst for being.

There are religious people who postulate the ages that are to come, speculate on these ages, and enunciate dogmas in relation to them that they propose in various forms, in forty-four forms. This is the experience of people who do not know, who do not see; this is the fervor and the contortion of people in prey to the thirst for being.

A skilled fisherman, or even a beginning fisherman, casts a net with dense webbing into a small pond, saying: "No matter what size the fish in this pond, they will be taken by my net." And when the fish are taken, the more they writhe they more they become entangled in the net. So it is with the religious people who speculate on the first ages, and on the ages to come, and on all their arguments. Without knowing, without seeing, in prey to the thirst for being, the more they writhe the more they become entangled in the net of their words.

As all the mangoes attached to a branch share the fate of the branch if it is broken, thus my body has broken all that leads to rebirth. As long as my body lasts, everyone will be able to see me. When it will die after having consumed all its life, no one will see it again.

From the Samannaphalasuttam Dutiyam

The monk will be fully satisfied with a robe that covers his body and a cup for the alms that will go to fill his belly. Wherever he goes, he gets along with everyone. Thus like a bird that flies with all its feathers wherever it goes, a monk with his robe and cup for alms takes all his belongings with him wherever he goes. With these, the monk is fully satisfied.

The monk is shorn of all desire of the world, he lives with a spirit freed of desire, his thoughts are completely purified of desire. He is freed from all wickedness and

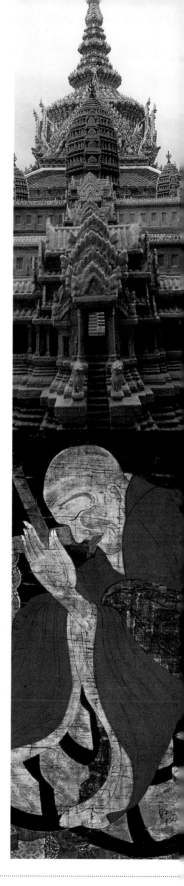

all corruption, lives thoughts free of evil, eager to do good to all living things. He is free of lethargy and from sloth. He has a vision of light, aware of himself, understanding. He keeps his thoughts pure and lives without anxiety, fully at peace, his mind free of doubt, without perplexity, in contact with good things.

Equipped with that noble treasure that is morality—a noble defense against difficulties—and the noble awareness of himself, of understanding, of absolute satisfaction, the monk selects a home set apart and in solitude, at the foot of a tree, or a mountain, or a steep cliff, or a cave, in a cemetery, a wood, on open ground, on a bundle of straw. There he sits after his meal, when he returns from gathering alms, his legs crossed, his body held upright, and there he reawakens the awareness of himself.

The monk is freed from the desire of the world, lives with a spirit freed of desire, and purifies his thoughts of all desire. He is freed from all wickedness and all corruption, he is eager to do good to all living things. He is free of lethargy and from sloth. He has an awareness of the light, is aware of himself, understanding. He is free of all anxiety and remorse, he has no doubts, no perplexity.

The monk experiences a sense of joy and well-being similar to that of the man who, having put himself in debt though an undertaking, sees the undertaking thrive in such a way as to repay the debt and leave earnings with which to buy gifts for his wife, and thus experiences a sense of joy and well-being for having earned and for having repaid the debt.

The monk experiences a sense of joy and well-being similar to that of the man who, having been sick and seriously suffering, so bad off that food meant nothing to him and his body was without strength, is finally freed from this indisposition and, with a feeling of joy and well-being, exclaims, "I was sick, but my body has regained its strength."

The monk experiences a sense of joy and well-being similar to that of the man who, having been put in prison, after a certain time is set free and finds himself safe and sound back among his belongings and experiences a sense of joy and well-being.

The monk experiences a sense of joy and well-being similar to that of the man who, having been held in slavery, unable to do as he pleased, unable to go where he wanted, after a certain time is set free and experiences a sense of joy and well-being.

The monk experiences a sense of joy and well-being similar to that of the rich man who, forced to travel with his goods through a dangerous and difficult jungle, as soon as he has reached the other side unharmed experiences a sense of joy and well-being. The monk who is freed from the five obstacles experiences joy in himself; from joy comes happiness; and when one is happy his body is calm, when his body is calm he feels well-being, and when he feels well-being his mind calms. He moves away from desire and wickedness and reaches the first stage of meditation, the result of detachment, thus leading to decisive reasoning and reflection, well-being and happiness. His body is then completely filled with the spirit of well-being.

The monk who has put an end to decisive reasoning and reflection reaches the second stage of meditation, when having calmed his inner being and concentrated his thinking, he excludes decisive reasoning and reflection and, as a result of meditation, finds happiness and well-being. His body is then completely filled with the spirit of well-being.

The monk, having achieved well-being, breaks with well-being and lives in indifference, aware, understanding, sensing serenity in his body. The nobles thus say he is indifferent; the aware say he is one who lives well. He thus achieves the third stage of meditation and is completely flooded with this well-being, without happiness.

When a monk frees himself from happiness and suffering, when he abolishes well-being and interior unease, in the absence of happiness and suffering, completely purified by indifference and by awareness of the self, he reaches the abode of the fourth stage of meditation. Seated, flooded by a pure thought, completely pure, he reaches one of the most beautiful and sublime states.

When a monk's thinking is completely concentrated, completely pure, clean, spotless, agile, ready to act, he directs himself toward the vision of Awareness. He knows then that his body, which has a form composed of four elements, created by a father and by a mother, is a mass of boiled rice and semolina, an impermanent thing, which by necessity will be consumed, crushed, broken, demolished, and even so his consciousness, which is his, is attached to it, chained to it.

When a monk's thinking is concentrated, pure, clean, spotless, agile, active, stabile, impassive, he can direct himself toward achievement of the spiritual principle. His body then produces another body, with a spiritual form, with all the faculties intact; thus, as the sword is drawn from the scabbard, there is awareness of what is the scabbard and what is the sword.

When the thinking of the monk is concentrated, pure, clean, immaculate, agile, active, stabile, impassive, he can direct himself toward the achievement of

marvelous powers, which he will sense within himself. Being one he becomes many, multiplied he becomes one; he can become visible or invisible, can pass at will through a wall or fence or hill as though through air; he can pass in and out of solid earth, can walk on the water's surface or glide through the air in a seated position as readily as a bird flies using its wings. He can take the moon and the sun into his hand and touch them—these two marvelous, important beings—and with his body he can extend his will even into the world of the Brahman.

When the thinking of the monk is concentrated, pure, clean, immaculate, agile, active, stabile, impassive, he can use his mind and direct it toward the plane of celestial hearing, which transcends the human, and he can hear both sounds, the human and the divine, these nearby, those distant. He can use his mind and direct it toward the penetration of the minds of others. He can direct it toward knowledge of the memories of preceding lives, toward knowledge of the death and the rebirth of all things. Finally, he can direct it toward awareness of the end of Evil, and all this is the sublime fruit of the state of the monk.

How were the various residences in previous lives? It is like someone who goes from his village to another, then from that to yet another, then from that he returns to his own village. And he says, "I went from my village to that, and there I stayed, I sat down, I spoke, and I sat in silence, in that and that other way; and then from that village I went to another, and then to another from which I came back to village."

Those who take poor care of their body, or their word, or their spirit, who insult the right, who are false and act accordingly, after death, when their body will break apart, they will be reborn on a bad route, moving toward decadence, ruin, and suffering.

Those that take good care of their body, of their word, of their spirit, those who do not insult the right, have a clear view, and act accordingly, after death, when their body will break apart, they will be reborn on the good path, moving toward the world of the sky. Thus the monk who has achieved celestial, purified vision, transcends the human and sees the beings that lose their existence and are reborn, sees the beings that are low and those that are high, the beautiful and the ugly, the happy and unhappy, according to the acts they perform.

For he who possesses knowledge and virtue, the word *caste* no longer exists, the word *family* no longer exists, the word *pride* no longer exists. He does not say, "You are my equal," or "You are not my equal." All those who are not attached to the caste, to family, to pride, to the creation of suitable marriages have reached the incomparable possession: knowledge and virtue.

From the Ambaththasuttam Tatiyam

People give themselves to pleasure, are enchanted by pleasure, are delighted by pleasure. The beings that behave in this way understand little of the law of the conditions or the original dependence of all things. Equally incomprehensible to them are the end of all formations, the abandonment of every cause for rebirth, the end of desire, detachment, cessation, the Annihilation [nirvana].

What is the aggregation of the corporeal form? There are the four primordial elements and the corporeal forms derived from them; and the four primordial elements are the solid element, the fluid element, the element of heat, and the element of vibration.

Even if a man possesses eyes, and even if those eyes are intact, if no external form enters his field of vision and no temporal connection takes place, no aggregation corresponding to conscious awareness is produced. Therefore I say: the awakening of awareness depends on certain conditions, and without those conditions no awareness can be awakened.

According to the conditions that can be produced, and without which no awareness can be awakened, the conditions can be defined thus: awareness of the eye, whose awakening depends on vision and on forms; awareness of the ear, whose awakening depends on hearing and on sounds; awareness of smell, whose awakening depends on the sense of smell and on odors; awareness of the tongue, whose awakening depends on taste and on flavors; awareness of the body, whose awakening depends on bodies and on contact; awareness of the spirit, whose awakening depends on the spirit and on the ideas.

From the Digha Nikaya

Pain that proceeds from this or that loss or misfortune that we must endure, torment, fear, secret displeasure, secret distress: this is what is meant by suffering.

Everything that because of one or another loss or misfortune that we must endure produces trembling and suffering and a miserable and distressed state: this is what is meant by lamentation.

Unpleasant physical suffering, the painful and unpleasant sensation produced by a physical contact: this is what is called pain.

Mental anguish that is unpleasant, the sad and unpleasant sensation produced by a mental contact: this is what is called sorrow.

The poisoning and the anguish that arise from one or another loss or misfortune that we must endure: this is what is called desperation.

Beings subject to birth say, "Oh, if only we could avoid being subject to new births!" Being subject to old age, to disease, to death, to suffering, to lamentations, to pain, to anguish, to desperation, they hope to free themselves, but that cannot be obtained with hope alone, and failing to obtain what one wants is also suffering.

The five aggregations tied to attachment are the corporeal form, the sensation, the perception, the mental forms, and awareness.

From the Samyutta Nikaya

Every material form, whether personal or external, crude or subtle, high or low, distant or near, belongs to the aggregation of the corporeal form tied to attachment.

Which do you believe is larger, the flood of tears you have shed in your long lives while rushing through the cycle of rebirths, joined to what you did not want and separated from what you wanted, or the waters of the four Oceans?

For a long time you have suffered for the death of your father, or your mother, or your sons, or your daughters, or your brothers, or your sisters. And while you suffered all this, tell me with sincerity, did it never occur to you that in this long time you have shed more tears than all the water contained in the four Oceans?

Which do you think is more abundant: the flood of blood that your mutilated body has shed along the long time of your life or the waters of the four Oceans? In truth, the number of you that, surprised like thieves or vagabonds or adulterers, have shed your blood along lengths of so many rebirths is so great that the amount of blood is far more than the waters contained in the four Oceans.

The beginning of the continuous transmigration cannot be discerned. It is impossible to discover the origin of this movement in which beings blinded by ignorance, duped by desire, have plunged en masse, giving rise to the wheel of rebirths. And thus, era after era, you have undergone suffering and torment and misfortune, you have filled cemeteries and cemeteries, enough in truth to be weary of every form of existence, enough to finally get away from it, be free of it.

Every sensation belongs to the aggregation of sensation. Every perception belongs to the aggregation of perception. Every mental formation belongs to the aggregation of mental formations. Every awareness belongs to the aggregation of awareness.

All aggregations are transitory, all aggregations are subject to suffering, all aggregations are entities with an ego. Form is transitory, sensation is transitory, perception is transitory, mental aggregates are transitory, awareness is transitory, and all that is transitory is subject to suffering, to perpetual change, and therefore no one can truly say, "This belongs to me, I am this, this is my self."

Think of a man who looks out over the full length of the Ganges in its course and who observes it with care. After having observed it with care it appears empty to him, unreal, without substance. In the same way the monk contemplates forms, sensations, perceptions, mental aggregates, and states of awareness, both of the past and the present, the near future and the far. He observes them, examines them closely, and after having examined them closely they appear empty to him, without ego, as nothing.

He who takes pleasure in a corporeal form, in sensations, in perceptions, in mental aggregates, or in awareness, takes pleasure in suffering, and he who takes pleasure in suffering will never be free of it.

What delight, what happiness, can there ever be in a place where everything has been burned? Wrapped in obscurity do you perhaps seek a light? Observe this puppet, this repugnant mass, diseased, full of desire, no part of which is destined to endure. The form is fragile; it is a nest of disease and decay: a body decays within a certain period, and death is the end of life.

From the Anguttara Nikaya

Have you ever seen, in this low world, a man or a woman of eighty, ninety, or a hundred years? Fragile, bent like a roof beam, leaning forward, supported by a cane, walking with uncertain steps, ill, all youth having long since fled, toothless, with thin hair or none at all, with wrinkled skin and knotty members. Did not the thought hit you that you too will be subject to decrepitude and that you will never be able to flee it?

Have you ever seen, in this low world, a sick man or woman, afflicted, dangerously struck, lying in his or her own excrement, unable to rise without the help of others, put to bed by others? Did you not think that you too will be subject to illness and that you will never be able to escape it?

Have you ever seen, in this low world, the cadaver of a man or a woman, two or three days after death, swollen, decomposed, completely rotten? Did not the thought come to you that you too are subject to death and that you will never be able to escape it?

The Texts of the Buddha and Buddhism: An Ocean of Pages

Just as the figure of Budda was multiplied into an endless number of divine images, the sermons he gave led to the creation of a vast literature. A multitude of writers presented the biography of the Buddha and explained his theories while also narrating the history and developments of Buddhism. Numerous Buddhist centers were opened in Europe, and these provided periodical publications of their own. It would not be wrong to state—bearing in mind that paper and printing existed in China as early as the first century after Christ—that more words have been written on Buddhism or in works related to Buddhism than on any other subject, and this during a period that covers roughly two thousand years.

Several highlights:

The oldest printed book that has been handed down to us is a ninth-century Chinese version of the Diamond Sutra printed from tabular woodcuts. The British Museum in London has a copy.

The Buddhist university of Nalanda—attended by 8,500 students and 1,500 teachers every year—also dates to the ninth century; preserved in its library, once considered the richest in the world, was a copy of every lesson (one hundred lessons were given every day).

In 1905, R. J. Jackson and J. R. Pain opened a library in London dedicated to Buddhist texts in English, the first such institution in the West for a non-Christian religion.

The common origin of every text was the canon in Pali, compiled between the first and second Buddhist council. It is divided in three parts (*Tipitaka*, meaning "three *pitaka*," a term that means "basket" or "collection of writings"); the Sutta Pitaka ("Basket of Discourses"), or collection of the Buddha's sermons divided into five volumes, with more than four thousand sutras; the Vinaya Pitaka ("Basket of Monastic Discipline"), which contains the rules of the order and is divided into three books; and the Abhidhamma Pitaka ("Basket of Scholastic Doctrine"), which deals with metaphysics, its seven treatises presenting the philosophy and science of the Buddha.

One of the most important commentaries on the Tipitaka books was written by Buddhaghosa, the Visuddhimagga ("Path of Purity"). Closely related to what the Buddha actually said is the Dhammasukkaya ("Compendium of the Law") by Avalokitasima, a collec-

Tibetan monks studying religious texts.

tion of aphorisms in several volumes, drawn from the Saddharma-smrty-upasthana-sutra and immediately spread in Sanskrit, Tibetan, and Chinese.

Bearing in mind that these texts reflect a few hundred years of oral tradition and manual transcription, along with the dogmatic diversifications that have resulted from the various schools of Buddhism, these canonical texts nonetheless can be taken to present reliable approximations of what the Buddha actually said. Complete certainty is not possible, of course. Aside from the Tipitaka, the Smaller Vehicle considers postcanonical the Milindapanha ("Questions of Menander"). The Greater Vehicle adds many other texts in Sanskrit to the canon, including the Mahavatsu and the Divyavadana. In Tibet monks read the Kanjur (108 volumes) and the Tanjur (250 volumes), aside from the Mahamunda of the first Tashi-Lama and treatises on occult science, such as the Kui-ti (35 volumes of text and 14 of commentary). Every sect has made its own large contribution to the already vast original literature of Buddhism.

The general contents of the Pali canon:

1. SUTTA PITAKA
("Basket of Discourses")

I   Digha Nikaya
     (34 sutras: "Group of Long Discourses")

II   Majjhima Nikaya (152 sutras: "Group of
     Medium-Length Discourses")

III Samyutta Nikaya (56 groups of sutras:
     "Group of Connected Discourses")

IV   Anguttara Nikaya (more than 2,500 sutras:
     "Group of Discourses Arranged Numerically
     in Ascending Order")

V   Khuddaka Nikaya
     ("Group of Small Texts")

1) Kuddakapatha, "small lessons"
2) Dhammapada, "verses of the law"
3) Udana, "verses of exaltation"
4) Itivuttaka, "so it was said"
5) Suttanipata, "collection of aphorisms"
6) Vimanavatthu, "the divine palaces"
7) Petavatthu, "the deceased"
8) Theragatha, "chants of monks"
9) Terigatha, "chants of female monks"
10) Jataka, "birth stories"
11) Niddesa, "index"
12) Partisambhidamagga, "the path of complete
     discrimination"
13) Apadana, "the undertakings"
14) Buddhavamsa, "the family of the Buddhas"
15) Cariyapitaka, "the basket of behavior"

2. VINAYA PITAKA
("Basket of Monastic Discipline")

I Suttavibhanga "division of the texts"
     1 Mahavibhanga, "large division,"
     or Bikkhuvibhanga, "division concerning
     the monks"

II Khandhaka, "the branches"
  1) Mahavagga, "the large section"
  2) Cullavagga, "the small section"

III Parivara, "epitome of the Vinaya";
     or Parivarapatha, "lessons and guidelines"

3. ABHIDHAMMA PITAKA
("Basket of Scholastic Doctrine")

I Dhammasangani, "enumeration of phenomena"

II Vibhanga, "book of treatises"

III Kathavatthu, "points of controversy"

IV Puggalapannati, "description of individuals"

V Dhatukatha, "discussion of the elements"

VI Yamaka, "books of pairs"

VII Patthana, "book of relations"

Glossary

This short glossary of Buddhist terms gives the terms in Sanskrit followed (in parentheses) by Pali.

A

Abhasa: reflected luminosity, resemblance, reflection. A thing considered as part or means of a whole; objectivity; theophany.

Abhava: nonpresence; any important element in nirvana (nibbana) or in ethereal space (*akasha*).

Abhidharma (*abhidamma*): that which refers to the Dharma; metaphysics; the name of the third "basket" of texts of the Theravada school, which has a strongly philosophical character and contains a complete system for training the psyche.

Abhinaya: aesthetic means, the art of communicating through representations. The whole of the conventional gestures used in scenic dance (*nrtya*).

Abhisambodhi: perfect, total enlightenment. The enlightenment (from *bodhi*, "awakening") of the supreme Buddhas.

Abhiseka: the consecration of birth; an ancient rite of Indian kings. In Tantric Buddhism, the sprinkling of water on a neophyte as an initiation rite.

Acarya: "he who teaches by example"; in a community of Buddhist monks, the spiritual master who, together with a teacher (*upajjhaya, upadhyaya*), guides the novice (*samanera, sramana*) for at least ten years.

Acyuta sthana (*acutta thana*): the "immutable condition," also called nirvana.

Adhisthana (*adhitthana*): the first perfection; the decision to dedicate oneself to asceticism; the "grace" with which the Buddha resolves the karma of a human being regardless of merits or demerits.

Adibuddha: the supreme or primordial Buddha. The Buddha of the beginning, born of himself. In Tibetan Buddhism the figure is represented by the cosmic Buddha Vajrasattva (Vajradhara).

Aggregations: *see* Skandha.

Agni: a Vedic fire god incorporated in the pantheon of Buddhist Tantrism.

Also called Anala or Vajranala. Always red in color, he rides a goat or ram.

Ahimsa: not killing, not harming; a fundamental precept in Buddhism that leads to benevolence to all life forms.

Akasa: ether, space, air; also "light." It becomes the infinite, immaterial site of nirvana, with the value of "highest heaven."

Akrti: image, resemblance, external appearance.

Akshobhya: "imperturbable"; one of the five celestial Buddhas, the Jinas. Also called Cittesa as "master of thought" (*citta*). In Tibetan art he is presented with one face and two hands, or three faces and six hands, or with four faces and eight hands. The five celestial Buddhas are Akshobhya, Amitabha, Amoghasiddha, Ratnasambhava, and Vairochana.

Alayavijnana: container of consciousness (*vijnana*). A sort of personal spirit in which are registered all the actions on the basis of which one will be recompensed. In the Yogachara school, it is cosmic awareness that encloses all the elements or seeds (*bija*) of every possible reality, a concept that is inconceivable to the human mind.

Alekhya: painting; *thangka* in Tibetan.

Amida: The Buddha as an incarnation of compassion, a spiritual principle of great importance to the Pure Land school.

Amitabha: "infinite light"; one of the five celestial Buddhas, the Jinas. Also called Amitayusu or Arolika or Vagisa ("lord of the word"). In Tibetan art he is presented with one face and two hands or one face and four hands or three faces and six hands or four faces and eight hands. The five celestial Buddhas are Akshobhya, Amitabha, Amoghasiddha, Ratnasambhava, and Vairochana.

Amoghasiddha: "infallible power," he whose action is not vain, whose action is incorruptible; one of the five celestial Buddhas, the Jinas. Also called Amogha, Amoghavajra, Dundhubhisavara, or Visvosnisa. In Tibetan art he is shown with one face and two hands, or with one face and four hands, or with three faces and six hands or with four faces and eight

hands. The five celestial Buddhas are Akshobhya, Amitabha, Amoghasiddha, Ratnasambhava, and Vairochana.

Amrta (*amata*): the outstanding absence of mortality that is an aspect of nirvana.

Anagarika: homeless. Applied to those who embrace the monastic life without becoming members of a monastery.

Ananda (also a proper name): the essence of joy, the principle of happiness, spiritual ecstasy.

Ananda-cin-maya: union of beatitude and reason. The state that characterizes an aesthetic experience (to taste the flavor: *rasasvadana*).

Anapana-smrti (*anapana-sati*): profound attention to the phenomenon of breathing, breathing in (*ana*) and breathing out (*apana*). A principal Buddhist practice, used to acquire *prana*. It is one of the Sixteen Contemplations.

Anatman (*anatta*): the "non-self," a Buddhist teaching that rejects the notion of an intrinsic, unchanging entity at the core of a person. It is one of the "three marks of existence," the others being *anitya* and *duhkha*.

Anitya (*anicca*): "impermanence," a characteristic of the flow of existence. One of the "three marks of existence."

An-upadi-sesa: not remaining, the condition of *nirupadhi-shesa-nibbana*. In assonance with *anupadha*: to be without a penultimate, applied to a letter or syllable that is not preceded by another.

Anuvyanjana: secondary physical signs of the Buddha or of bodhisattvas, chaktravartins, and mahapurushas (the primary auspicious attributes or marks are the *lakshanas*).

Apsaras (*atthara*): angelic beings or celestial nymphs, companions of the *gandharva* (heavenly musicians). One of the primary motifs in the iconography of the sky in Tibetan and Chinese Buddhist art. According to some, they appear to ascetics, who attempt to keep them from disturbing meditation.

Arhat (*arhant*): "worthy one." The saint "who has done what was to be done" (*krta-karaniya, katakaranlya*). The ideal wise man of Hinayana (Theravada) Buddhism; in initiation schools the name indicates the fourth stage on the path of evolution (*shrotapanna*).

Aryan: term used, perhaps inappropriately, for the peoples who invaded India around 1500 BC, supplanting the indigenous Indus Valley civilization. The Aryans established a social organization based on four castes: priests (Brahmans); warriors or nobles (Ksatriyas); artisans, farmers, and merchants (Vaisyas); and the subject people (Sudras). In Buddhism the word indicates a person whose moral sense leads him to follow the way of the Dharma with the Four Noble Truths (*aryasatyani, ariyasaccani*).

Aryasatyani (*ariyasaccani*): the Four Noble Truths, which are the existence of pain (*duhkha, dukkha*), the origin of pain (*duhkha-samudaya*), the extinction of pain (*duhkha-nirodha*), and the way that leads to that extinction (*marga, magga*).

Asamskrta: the not composite, not aggregate; an outstanding attribute of the heaven of nirvana (*akasa*) and of nirvana (*nibbana*) itself.

Ashram: the dwelling located in a secluded spot to which the yogi or Hindu sage withdraws for meditation. The word also applies to a group of disciples instructed in such a setting.

Ashtamangala: the "eight jewels," of Buddhism (in Tibetan *bkra-shis rTags brGyad*). The primary ornaments in all Buddhist iconography, in particular that of the Greater Vehicle school. In Tibetan Buddhism the eight jewels are impersonated by divinities. The eight jewels are the parasol (*chattra*; in Tibetan *Rin-chen gDugs*), which protects from demons; the two golden fish (*survana matsya*; in Tibetan, *gSer-gyi Nya*), symbolic of salvation from the ocean of rebirths and pain; the conch shell (*shankha*; in Tibetan, *Dung-dKar gYas-hKhyil*), which proclaims the glory of the saints; the cylindrical banner (*dhvaja*, in Tibetan, *mChog-gyi rGyal-mTshan*), which celebrates the victory of the Buddha; the intertwined or endless knot (*shrivatsa*, in Tibetan, *dPal-gyi Behu*), also called the Knot of Love; the vase of great treasures (*kalasha*, in Tibetan, *gTer-chen-pohi Bum-pa*), which contains spiritual jewels; the lotus flower (*padma*, in Tibetan, *Pad-ma bZang-po*); and the wheel (*chakra*, in Tibetan, *gSer-gyi hKhor-lo*), or the wheel of the law put in motion by the Buddha.

Ashtanga-marga (*atthangika-*

magga): The Eightfold Path composed of right faith, right will, right speech, right action, right livelihood, right effort, right mindfulness, and right concentration.

Asubha: absence of impurities; purity. One of the five stops (*bhavana*) in the ascent to the self.

Atman; atma (*atuma; atta*): the innermost self, the concept of the individual self; the term can be taken to refer to the concept of the soul, which is, however, denied by canonical Buddhism. The Hindu concept also includes the *jovatma, anuatma,* and *vijnam brahman*.

Aupadesika: to acquire through instruction; he who has acquired the ability to understand the aspects of things through study.

Avalokiteshvara: "the lord that looks from above," one of the great bodhisattvas (Chinese Kuanj-yin; Japanese Kannon). Also called Lokeshvara, Lokanatha. He appears in a variety of forms in Buddhist iconography, almost always associated with his function as gatherer of souls to bring them to heaven; as a result he is often presented as a female bearing a child in her arms. He can have one face and two hands, one face and six hands, one face and eight hands, three faces and six hands, five faces and twelve hands, but also—in unorthodox votive images—many overlapping faces and an abundance of hands.

Avandana: exegesis, narration of the meritorious acts performed by past Buddhas or by historical Buddhas during their preceding lives and their incarnation in this life.

Avastha: the minimal condition of elements that aggregate to compose a being both physical and psychic.

Avasthana: an emotional condition or situation.

Avidya (*a-vijja*): nonconsciousness, the ignorance that is the cause of existence in the world, which is illusory and fleeting. It is the first of the Twelve Links of Conditioned Existence (Twelve Nidanas) and the last of the Ten Bonds. Because of ignorance the individual sees the world as real and fails to see his or her transitory nature. In more esoteric Buddhist schools it is given the same value as the illusion (*maya*) to which the supreme law (Dharma) ascribes the origin of the world of forms, which is conditional and illusory.

Ayatana: name for the twelve

containers of the senses, six of which, internal or subjective (*adhayatmika, ajhatika*), involve the five senses plus mental perception; the other six are external and relate to the objects of the senses and to things, since they are conceived by the mind.

Ayuksamskara (*ayusankhara*): vital structures essential to the living individual and to the Buddha, which are rejected at the moment of the extinction that is nirvana.

B

Bhakti: "devotion," abandonment to love. One of the five principles of Hindu yoga, based on the devotion and love for an ideal that has no trace of self-interest or philosophical speculation, such as the sentiment that drove the Buddha to preach the Dharma to humanity. In treatises on ethics it is the equivalent of a *lakshana*, meaning a sign of the Buddha, and is synonymous with *dhvani*, meaning "contents."

Bhava: existence. One of the twelve causal factors that effect the flow of transmigrations (*samara*).

Bhâva: nature, emotion, mystical state, sentiment, or state of mind produced by the contemplation of a work of art. A condition of existence in the world and an innate property of the minimal elements called dharmas.

Bhavana: creation; production; imagination, the persistence or emotional impression that survives in the memory; the act of internal visualization of objects that occurs in meditation. According to the school, there are either three *bhavanas* (*kaya-, citta-,* and *prajna-bhavana*) or five, in which case they serve to achieve the four cardinal virtues: benevolence (*maitri*), joy (*mudita*), compassion (*karuna*) and equanimity (*upeksa*), plus purity (*a-subha*).

Bhikshu (*bhikkhu*): Buddhist monk, mendicant, ascetic; synonym: *sramana*. A Buddhist nun is *bhikshuni* (*bhikkuni*).

Bhumi: earth, ground, and also a stage of spiritual attainment or perfection. There are ten (or twelve) such stages of perfection, indicating the gradual approach of a bodhisattva to the state of the awakening mind (*bodhicitta*). The primary ones are generosity (*dana*), morality (*sila*), patience (*skanti*), vigor (*virya*), meditation (*dhyana*), and achievement of wisdom (*prajna*). In

Tibetan Buddhism the ten (or twelve) stages have been deified and are presented in the persons of gods with characteristic colors: Sdhimukticarya (zealous conduct; red); Pramudita (the festive; red); Vimala (the immaculate; white); Prabhakari (the sparkling; red); Arcismati (the radiant; green); Sudurjaya (the invincible; yellow); Abhimukhti (he who confronts; gold); Durangama (he who goes far; black or blue); Acala (the immobile; white); Sadhumati (of good intelligence; white); Dharmamegha (cloud of law; yellow); Samantaprabha (who shines everywhere; the color of the sun at noon; also shown as the Buddha Amitabha on a lotus flower). The term appears in the word *bhumisparshamudra*, the Buddha's gesture of "touching earth to call on it as witness."

Bhutatathata: "that," the "being such," the essence of all matter. Synonym: *Tathata*.

Bija: seed; the elements of every possible reality contained in the cosmic container of consciousness (*alayavijnana*).

Bimba: model, theme, subject. Presenting oneself as one is, with one's own features.

Bodhi: the awakening, enlightenment, thanks to which—having eliminated the thirst to live and ignorance—one reaches the state of awareness that preludes the total extinction that will end in death.

Bodhianga (*bojjhanga*): the seven requisites that make possible the achievement of enlightenment (*bodhi*). These are awareness, effort, energy, joy, calm, contemplation, and equanimity.

Bodhicitta: awareness, the awakening mind. In the Mahayana school it is the quality intrinsic in every being, thanks to which extinction will become possible as soon as the being begins to actively work to achieve it.

Bodhipaksika (*bodhipakkhika*): "wings of enlightenment," or the thirty-seven predispositions or psychic elements that prepare for the achievement of enlightenment.

Bodhisattva (*bodhisatta*): an "enlightenment being," a potential Buddha; one who, although living in this world, is destined to become a Buddha in the next rebirth. This concept was later applied to one who, having reached the threshold of nirvana, returns to earth to help other human beings. In the Mahayana

school, bodhisattvas are emanations of the Buddha that provide spiritual assistance in his mission. Twenty-four bodhisattvas are identified, divided in several groups; but these can take on up to a hundred personifications.

Bodhi tree (Bo tree, *Bodhivrksa*, *Bodhirukka*): the pipal tree under which Siddhartha Gautama attained enlightenment. Considered the center of the world, it is located today—as a result of replantings—on the site of the historical enlightenment in Bodha Gaya, India.

Bon or Pon: an indigenous religion of Tibet, based on the worship of natural forces, that had an influence on Buddhism when it arrived in Tibet.

Bonze (*bonzo*): Japanese term for Buddhist monk.

Brahma, Brahmaji: Hindu divinity integrated into the pantheon of Buddhist Tantrism with various functions and thus with a variety of appearances. In Vedantism he is the first being created in the universe, which, thanks to powers granted by the supreme god, created all things and rules them. He is one of the twelve great divinities (*mahajana*) and is the god of passion (*rajo-guna*).

Brahman: Hindu priest, member of the first of the four Aryan castes. In Buddhism the term is applied to those who follow the way of the Dharma and to a saint (arhat).

Buddha: from *bodhi*, "enlightenment." The Enlightened One, the Awakened. All the enlightened ones who in every era (*yuga*, *kapla*) achieve full awareness of the Dharma and teach it to humanity are Buddhas. The last fully humanized Buddha (*Manusi-Buddha*) was Gautama Shakyamuni (Gotama Sayyamuni); the next Buddha will be *Maitreya* (*Metteyya*), currently a bodhisattva in Tushita heaven. There are also Buddhas that do not preach to humanity (*Pratyeka-Buddha*). Synonym: *Tathagata*. In Tantric Buddhism the term is rarely applied to the historical Buddha but instead to the celestial divinities (Jinas) that are sacred to the cardinal points (six). These five celestial Buddhas are Aksobhya, Amitabha, Amoghasiddha, Ratnasambhava, and Vairochana; a sixth is sometimes added to these, Vajrasattva (Vajradhara), who rules over all of them.

Buddhi: the psyche, the intellect in its quality of reflection and judgment. Synonyms: *manas*, *citta*.

C

Caitya (*cetiya*): receptacle, reliquary. Originally used for the earth used to cover a burial; also used to indicate the stupa, or *dagoba*.

Chakravartin (*cakkhavattin*): those who set in motion the wheel of the Dharma; a name applied to the universal monarchs of ancient Indian tradition, relatively similar to the historical Buddha (*Manusi-Buddha*).

Ch'an: Chinese name for Zen, derived from the Sanskrit word *dhyana* ("meditation").

Chela: follower or disciple of a Hindu master, or guru.

Citta: awareness, the universal principle of active intelligence, understood as fundamental to authentic existence.

Citta-vrtti: mental fluctuation; fleeting emotions or material images.

Civara: the robe of a Buddhist monk.

D

Dakini: she who walks in space. In Tibetan Buddhism this is a category of minor gods, along with the *yogini*. It is also the tutelary Shakti of the *muladharachakra*.

Dalai Lama: Mongolian term, *dalai*, that translates the Tibetan *gyamtso*: "ocean"; the spiritual head of Lamaism, Tibetan Buddhism, considered an incarnation of the Buddha Avalokiteshvara, protector of the Buddha. His temporal power dates to 1742, and since 1959 the Dalai Lama has lived in exile. He is elected on the basis of the ascertainment of the presence of the "signs" of the Buddhist divinity.

Deva: "the shining"; divinity primarily of the Hindu pantheon that has the role of ruling a sector of material creation and providing the necessities for all beings. In Buddhism, *devas* are divine beings as a result of meritorious actions; they inhabit celestial realms but are still subject to rebirth unless they continue to perform meritorious actions.

Dhana, dhyana (*jhana*): meditation, mystical ecstasy. It is divided in four stages of progressive growth; also the path of Buddhist asceticism leading to awareness of absolute reality; in Chinese it is Ch'an, in Japanese Zen.

Dharma (*dhamma*): term with many meanings. It is the law, norm, or doctrine revealed by the Buddha in keeping with the Four Noble Truths; it is the reality of things; in the plural, it refers to the minimal elements of physical and psychic reality and of intuitive thought. Although insignificant by themselves, aggregations of these dharmas are the origin of human existence, which is a result of actions performed in preceding lives.

Dharma-chakra-pravartana (*dhamma-cakka-pavattana*): the act of setting in motion the wheel of the law, or the revelation of the Dharma by the Buddha in his sermon at Benares (Varanasi).

Dharmadhimukti: a calling for the Dharma.

Dharmkaya: the objective essentiality of the Dharma.

Dharmshunyata: the "emptiness" (*shunyata*) of the minimal elements that compose the reality of the individual.

Dhatu: "base"; the eighteen spheres of action, three to each *ayatana*. The steps of ascent according to psychic disposition from the sphere of desire to the annihilation of nirvana.

Dhyai: to meditate on, to concentrate on; also, to contemplate abstractly, together with the Vedic term *dhi*.

Dikpala: Brahman divinity incorporated into the pantheon of Tibetan Buddhism in which it has been multiplied into eight or ten *dikpala*, serving functions as guardians of various regions of space.

Divya-caksus (*dibba-cakkhu*): the so-called third eye or divine spiritual insight with which the Buddha, as he was about to achieve enlightenment, was able to contemplate the Twelve Links of Conditioned Existence (Twelve Nidanas) and the relationships among all past, present, and future beings.

Dorje: In Tibetan Buddhism the symbol of lightning, used in art and in magical ritual practices. In Sanskrit, *vajra*.

Duhkha (*dukkha*): pain, unhappiness. The first of the Four Noble Truths (*arya-satyani*) and with *anatmaka* and *anitya* one of the "three marks of existence."

Dvesa (*dosa*): hatred, malevolence, aversion. One of the five (or ten) moral afflictions or poisons (*kleshas*) and one of the three fires that cause *duhkha*.

E

Eight Jewels: *See* Ashtamangala.

G

Garbhavakranti (*gabbhavakkanti*): the "descent of the seed," or the act

of physical incarnation of the historical Buddha in the body of Maya, wife of King Shuddhodana. One of the recurrent themes of Buddhist iconography beginning with Gandharan sculpture.

Garuda: winged devourer; fantastic bird based on the eagle. Found throughout Indian tradition; in Hinduism it is the great enemy of the Naga and the steed of the god Vishnu. Incorporated into the Tibetan Buddhist pantheon, it was assimilated with the fantastic bird Khyung, known to many cultures under many names.

Gatha: song; the verse portion of Buddhist texts (sutras).

Guna: a specific good quality of a work of art; a factor, quality, or qualification of the material world, such as *sattva-guna*, "purity," *rajo-guna*, "expansion, continuation," and *tamo-guna*, "inertia, resistance."

Guru: in Hinduism a religious guide, a master, or *swami*, who instructs the *chelas*.

H

Heruka, Hevajra: the luminous He, an important god in the pantheon of Tibetan Buddhism, usually presented in paintings at the center of cemeteries, surrounded by eight *yogini* or by sixteen divinities. Like Buddhakapala (the skullcap of the Buddha), he can be the center of a mandala. Like Mahamaya ("great Illusion"), he is especially frightening. Like Sambara ("constriction"), he crushes cadavers. Like Vajradaka, he is usually black. These figures can also become autonomous divinities and acquire greater iconographic variety.

Hinayana: the Lesser Vehicle (of salvation), the Theravada school of Buddhism, the oldest, most traditional, and perhaps most orthodox school of Buddhism.

I

Indra: in Hinduism the god of rain and lightning, king of the celestial planets, sovereign of the gods of the heavens. Incorporated into the Tibetan Buddhist pantheon he is usually painted yellow or gold and rides an elephant with six hooves. He is the guardian of the East. Other names: Purandana, Vajrayudha.

J

Jataka: "birth stories," canonical narrations of 550 events concerning

the life and acts of the Buddha in the incarnation that preceded Gautama.

Jati: birth, one of the twelve causal factors that determine the cycle of rebirths (*samsara*).

Jijimuge: the basic doctrine of the Japanese Kengon school. It preaches the free interfusion of absolute reality and each individual thing. It represents one of the heights reached by human philosophy, together with Sufism and Zen.

Jina: "victorious" (also *tathagata*, "he that is thus"). The Buddhas of the five cardinal points (south, east, north, west, and center); the five Jinas of Tibetan Buddhism are Vairochana (at the center or to the east, white, in the gesture of meditation, on a lion, with a wheel as attribute, accompanied by Locana; ruler of the material); Aksodhya (at the center or to the east, blue-black, in the gesture of touching the earth, on an elephant, with lightning as attribute, accompanied by Mamaki; ruler of awareness); Ratnasambhava (south, yellow, in the gesture of giving a gift, on a horse, with the jewel as attribute, accompanied by Mamaki; ruler of sensation); Amitabha (west, red, in the gesture of meditation, on a peacock, with the lotus as attribute, accompanied by Pandara; ruler of the intellect); Amoghasiddha (north, green, in the gesture of protection, on Garuda, with the sword or lightning as attribute, accompanied by Tara; ruler of karma). The term *Jina* is common to other Indian religions, in particular Jainism, which arose during the same period as Buddhism. In Nepal the Jinas are also called, improperly, Dhyani-Buddhas.

Jiriki: Japanese term indicating the individual effort needed to travel the path of salvation, as opposed to *tariki*, which refers to the intervention of an external savior.

Jivan-mukta: he who has reached spiritual freedom but still appears in human form.

Jodo: the Pure Land school as it developed in Japan. In this school, faith and good acts are equals in the path toward the achievement of salvation. It gave origin to the Shin school, which puts the accent exclusively on faith.

Jnana: awareness, one of the ten stages of spiritual attainment or perfection (*bhumi*). When the awareness is "superior" it is called mystical awareness, or prajna.

K

Kala: art, any artistic production or any work made with skill. There are sixty-four practical arts (*bahyakala*), some of which are identical to the professional arts (*silpa*), and also sixty-four "intimate arts," or "arts of love" (*abhyantara-kala*).

Kalpa (*kappa*): great cosmic age, divided in four or eight cycles (*yuga*). In Hinduism it is the duration of a single day for the Brahma, composed of 4,320 million earth years and including one thousand cycles of four eras (*maha-yuga*).

Kama: sensual desire, in particular lust. One of the passions (*raga*) that cause the chain of rebirths. Among the arts are sixty-four "intimate arts," or "arts of love" (*abhyantara-kala*).

Kapala: ritual cup carved from a human skullcap.

Karma (*kamma*): "deed or action"; the theory according to which positive (*punka-karman*) or negative (*papa-karman*) acts determine one's life situation in this and future lives. For this reason each human will be reborn in a more enlightened position if he or she performed meritorious acts in past lives; similarly, he or she will be born into a position of suffering as a result of having performed wicked acts. This doctrine of moral compensation is inseparable from that of reincarnation, and Buddhism shows the way to escape it and achieve total annihilation.

Karuna: "compassion"; one of the four cardinal virtues of the Buddha, which are compassion, loving kindness (*maitri*), pleasure in the joys of others (*mudita*), and equanimity (*upeksa*). In the Mahayana school, *karuna* and supreme wisdom (*prajna*) are the virtues necessary to reach enlightenment since every action performed in this world is unsubstantial since the world itself is unsubstantial.

Kausala: skill, ability. In Buddhism, if a skill is applied as a moral gift, it becomes an advantage.

Kavya: "poetry or poetic form" (in prose or verse). If distinct from specific religious compositions it is literature. In the abstract sense it can be taken as the equivalent of "art" hence, *kavitva-dayin*, "artistic."

Kaya: body, substance, perceptible existence. Both the Smaller and Greater vehicles of Buddhism attribute a physical body to the Dharma and have compiled a series of concepts concerning the existence of the theoretical reality of the Buddha and his function.

Kaya-vat-citta: "body-word-mind"; for the Mahayana school these are the three levels of physical, psychic, and mental manifestation. They correspond to the three mediums in which the cosmic Buddha manifests himself: actuation of the Dharma, participation, and manifestation.

Klesha (*kilesa*): moral affliction or poison that leads to karma and thus rebirth. There are variously five or ten *kleshas*: greed, hate, delusions, anxiety, heresy, doubt, laziness, arrogance, impudence, insensitivity.

Klista-mano-vijnana: awareness of contaminated intellectual will. Obscurely produced by ignorance (*avidya*), which makes one fall prey to moral afflictions (*kleshas*) and remain a prisoner to the cycle of rebirths (*samsara*) because of ignorance of the right awareness of universal reality (*alayavignana*).

Klrtimukha: an Indian decorative motif that in Tibetan art assumes the characteristic appearance of the terrifying mask of a monster.

Koan: from Japanese Zen Buddhism, a riddlelike story or account that cannot be understood by reason and can only be grasped by breaking through the boundaries of conditioning and prejudice to arrive at a form of enlightened seeing. Koans are used as exercises in freeing the mind from thought patterns.

Krodha: divinities in the pantheon of Tibetan Buddhism with enraged features that often serve as guardians of the access portals of a mandala. Four are listed but also eight can appear, and quite often ten.

Krta-karanlya (*katakaraniya*): he who has done what needed to be done, an arhat.

Ksana (*khana*): "instant," an infinitesimal measure of time.

Ksanti (*khanti*): patience or tolerance, one of the six, or ten, perfections (*paramitas*).

Ksatriya (*khattiya*): the caste of the warriors and nobles in the Aryan division of the classes in India (*varna*).

L

Lakshana (*lakkhana; lancana*): the outstanding characteristics of the minimal elements of physical reality; also the primary auspicious attributes or marks on the body of the Buddha as well as on bodhisattvas, chakravartins, and mahapurushas (the secondary physical signs are the *anuvyanjanas*).

Lama: a Lamaist monk; the prior of a monastery in Tibetan Buddhism.

Lantsa: the Tibetan system of writing, based on the Sanskrit *devanagari*.

Laukika: the things of the world (*loka*) that fall in the dominion of the "relative truth" (*samvrtti-satya*).

Lobha: greed, thirst, a synonym for the "overwhelming anger" of the Three Fires: passion (*raga*), hate (*dosa*), stupidity (*moha*).

Loka: world, sphere, universe; in a specific sense, the conditional world, the world of perceived reality.

Lokottara (*lokuttara*): the whole of reality, which, transcending the world of perceived reality, belongs to the sphere of absolute truth (*paramartha-satya*).

M

Madhyamaka: "middle"; in the Mahayana school of Buddhism, a system of reconciliation between the world of perceived reality, which is unreal but considered real as the empirical truth (*samvritti-satya*), and absolute truth (*paramartha-satya*), in the light of which the world seems completely unreal.

Madhyama pratipad (*majjhama patipada*): the "middle way" of Buddhist doctrine, so named by the Buddha because it is far from the extremes of both the ascetic life and the worldly life.

Madhyamika: Buddhist school that follows the Mahayana system of reconciliation, known as *madhyamaka*.

Mahapurusha (*mahapurisa*): "great man"; term from Vedic philosophy applied to a being gifted with extraordinary perfection; the idea is applied to a cosmic model proposed to humans and exemplified by the Buddha, bodhisattvas, and chakravartins.

Mahasidda: "great *siddha*," meaning "great saint"; one of the eighty-four Indian and Tibetan ascetics who were important in the creation of esoteric Tantric Buddhism.

Mahavira: "great hero"; name often given the great masters of Jainism and also to the Buddha.

Mahayana: the Great Vehicle. Name for northern Buddhism, with various schools of a mystical metaphysical trend and religious organization. The principal schools are the Madhyamika (or S'nyavada), the Vijnanavada (or

Yogachara); the Vajrayana Tantric schools; and the Sino-Japanese T'ien T'ai (Tendai), Ch'ing-tu, Shingon, and Zen schools. The most important is the Tibetan or Lamaist school.

Mahesvara: "great lord," the Hindu god Shiva, god of ignorance, dedicated to the destruction of the universe at the end of the life of Brahma, who generated him. Incorporated into the pantheon of Tibetan Buddhism, he is the guardian of the West. Also called Isana, Nilakantha, and Rudra.

Maitreya (*Metteya*): the benevolent; name of the Buddha of the future, to whom the sage Kashyapa transmitted the "dress," and with it the powers, of the Buddha. He will be incarnated on the earth in 2,500 years in a family of Brahmans. According to Tibetan Buddhism he is now living in Tushita heaven. In accordance with the quinary system that matches the last five incarnate Buddhas with the five Jinas, he corresponds to Amoghassiddha.

Maitri (*metta*): "loving kindness"; one of the four cardinal virtues of Buddhism, together with compassion (*karuna*), joy (*mudita*), and equanimity (*upeksa*). It is the subject of one of the most important books of Buddhism, the Maitri Sutra.

Manas: mental or intellectual; the organ that coordinates the functions of the senses as opposed to the awareness or wisdom (*vijnana*, *citta*) with which one reaches essential truth.

Mandala (*dKyil-'khor* in Tibetan): mystical-magical symbolic representation of the universe, usually as a circle. Typical of Tibetan Buddhism, it can be taken as a description of the plane of time, with various divinities (Tathagata, bodhisattvas, and others) at the cardinal points. These points are colored red for West, yellow for South, blue for East, and green for North. At the center is a sanctuary (*kutagara*) enclosing the sovereign divinity of the mandala (*mandalesha*) or the wheel (*chakresha*). The sanctuary is surrounded by one or more concentric galleries (*pattika*), sometimes divided in houses (*kosthaka*). The whole is enclosed and framed by a wall (*prakara*) with a portal (*torana*) at each of the four cardinal points. Sometimes the whole is contained in a protective circle in the image of the wheel (*chakra*). There are thirty-seven

different types of mandala.

Mantra (*manta*): from the Vedic "hymn or deliberation" (from *mana*, "mind," and *treaya*, "liberation"). The word originally referred to a sacred text or short prayer, an emblematic phrase, a formula. The constant repetition (*japa*) of a mantra (very often the name of a deity), with special phonetic stresses, is believed to lead to direct communication with the unconscious and to contemplation of esoteric truths, such as those expressed graphically by the symbols of a mandala. Such magical stanzas can be found, for example, in the Rig-Veda, which is a collection of hymns.

Manusi-Buddha: the historical Buddha; a Buddha who has become incarnated to accomplish his mission.

Mara: "Death"; enemy divinity of the Buddha and of all those who follow the path to liberation, whom he seeks to defeat by presenting the appeals of temporal life with the help of desire. In Tantric texts he represents the four obstacles that attempt to defeat the Buddha on the path to enlightenment: *klesha, skandha, mrtyu, and devaputra*. In Tibetan Buddhism these become four different Mara divinities, and certain Buddhist schools have matched these to the four Hindu divinities Brahma, Yaksa, Yama, and Indra.

Marici: "ray of dawn"; a highly important goddess in the pantheon of Tibetan Buddhism, where she is presented atop a pig or on a cart drawn by seven pigs. She is an assistant to the two Taras.

Maya: "that which is not"; illusion, which causes the unlearned to believe in the real world, which is transitory and insubstantial in space and time. Also the name of the Buddha's mother, also called Mahamaya.

Moha: stupidity or infatuation, one of the three principal moral infections, or Three Fires, the other two being passion (*raga*) and hate (*dosa*).

Moksa (*mokka*): liberation, spiritual freedom. Liberation from the chain of continuous rebirths; the "realization" of perfection.

Mondo: Japanese term indicating the rapid and absolute nature of the koans of Zen.

Mudita: joy, happiness at the joy of others. One of the four cardinal virtues of Buddhism, the other three being "loving kindness" (*maitri*), compassion (*karuna*), and equanimity (*upeksa*).

Mudra (*mudda*): "seal"; at first the use of the fingers to indicate a number (*hattha-mudda-ganana*); later every symbolic gesture using the hands, in particular in Indian dance. The gestures, or hand positions, of the Buddha indicate particular moments in his earthly life and also indicate the essence of those moments. In Tibetan Buddhism the word applies to the mate (wife-power: *sakti*) of a Tathagata or bodhisattva.

Mridanga (*mridangam*): Indian drum shaped like an elongated vase or barrel open at both ends, one opening smaller than the other, the openings covered in skin to form drums.

N

Naga: the cobra, or a serpent deity. The Naga occupied an important place in Indian tradition and were integrated into the pantheon of Tibetan Buddhism, usually numbering eight or ten.

Namarupa: "name-form"; word-image. The formation of an identity as a result of the actions (*karma*) accumulated (*upacita*) by a person during preceding lives. Also the conventional means of recognition, thanks to which we know the universe. It is the third of the Twelve Links of Conditioned Existence (Twelve Nidanas) that cause the chain of rebirths in the *pratlya-samutpada*.

Nat: nature spirits that predate the advent of Buddhism but are worshiped in Myanmar (Burma).

Nidana: "cord," primary cause. The Twelve Links of Conditioned Existence that cause the chain of rebirths are also called the Twelve Nidanas. They are presented as rays in the wheel of life. They are ignorance (*avidya*), aggregation (*samskaras*), reflective consciousness (*vijnana*), name-form (*nama-rupa*), the five senses plus the mental (*sadayatana*), contact or perception (*sparsa*), sensation (*vedana*), desire (*trsna*), attachment (*upadana*), existence (*bhava*), birth (*jati*) and old age-death (*jara-marana*).

Nikaya: "collection, mass"; name of the five great groups into which the Sutta Pitaka is divided.

Nirmanakaya: the "emanation body," the body of existential "manifestations," the body with which the Buddha appears incarnate, thus one of his three bodies (*trikaya*).

Nirodha: "end," a synonym for nirvana.

Nir-upadhi-sesa-nirvana: definitive and total extinction of every action, even those meritorious, which takes place with the physical death of a Buddha. It is the second phase of final extinction (nirvana), following the first, which is called *sopadhi-sesa-nirvana*. Compare *parinirvana*.

Nirvana (*nibbana*): the absolute annihilation or extinction of all causal connections (*pratityasamutpada*) that lead to rebirths (*samsara*). Enlightened awareness of the emptiness of the minimal elements whose aggregations lead to life. Absolute liberation from pain.

Nityabaddha: living things that are prisoners of the world and of the chains of rebirths because of the Twelve Links of Conditioned Existence.

Niyama: a consolidated rule; the primary restrictions in the practice of yoga leading to purity and virtue.

Nrtya: scenic dance, artistic dance.

P

Padma: the lotus (*Lotus nelumbium*); also called pundarika, utpala (*Lotus nymphea*).

Pali: one of the most ancient dialects of southern India, used for the writing of the Theravada canon and several other Buddhist texts. Perhaps based on the Maghadi dialect of northern India, although some scholars consider it an independent language confined to its religious use. The use of Pali declined in India with the decline of Buddhism, reflowering in the fourth century AD in Ceylon and again in the eleventh century in Myanmar. Pali is less ductile than Sanskrit, to which is it related, presenting various grammatical simplifications and phonetic assimilations (as for example in the Sanskrit *nirvana*, Pali *nibbana*; Sanskrit *arkah*, Pali *allo*). *See* Samskr.

Panchamudra: the Five Seals.

Pancharaksha: the Five Protectors, thus the five formulas (*dharani*) used in specific cases of need; in the pantheon of Tibetan Buddhism they are personified as five female divinities: Pratisara (protects from sin and illness); Sahasrapramardani (protects from demons); Mahamayuri (protects from snakes); Mantranusarini (protects against diseases); and Sitavati (protects against wild animals and dangerous insects). These names are often preceded by the term *maha* ("great").

Pandit: Vedic term used to indicate someone learned in the scriptures, thus a wise or learned man in general.

Pansil: an abbreviation of *pancha sila*; the Five Precepts, a name given to a recitation of the Theravada with which the reader promises to him- or herself to abandon the way of darkness.

Paramartha-satya (*paramatthasacca*): the truth (*satya*) of the absolute (*paramartha*). The absolute truth that transcends empirical truth (*samvrtti-satya*).

Paramita: "perfection"; the *paramitas* are the six or ten stages of spiritual attainment or perfection (*bhumi*) that the bodhisattva must develop in order to achieve enlightenment. These virtues are generosity, or liberation from the thirst for possessions (*dana*); morality (*sila*); patience (*ksanti*); vigor (*virya*); meditation (*dhyana*); and wisdom of reality (*prajna*). Within the pantheon of Tibetan Buddhism these perfections appear as twelve divinities, with names and specific colors and attributes, representing the perfection of the lotus and the jewel, charity; morality; patience; energy; meditation; wisdom; behavior; will; power; knowledge; and perfection.

Parardha: period that indicates the midlife of the Brahma (in the Vedic religion) or, in Tantric Buddhism, a *kalpa*, a period of 4,320 million x 2 x 30 x 12 x 50 years.

Paratantra: condition of non-autonomy that causes the minimal elements of physical reality (dharmas) to be chained together without their usual order; it also means the intuition of this condition.

Parikalpita: fallacious concept according to which the minimal elements of physical reality (dharmas) are considered themselves to be real.

Parinamana: the generous act by which a bodhisattva transfers to others merits he or she has acquired through a perfection (*adhistana*). The Mahayana doctrine of *parinamana* is called *parivarta*.

Parinirvana (*parinibbana*): total extinction—also of meritorious acts—following the death of a Buddha.

Parinnispanna: transcending the conditions of the minimal elements of physical reality (the dharmas), making possible achievement of an understanding of their absolute vacuity (*sunya-ta*).

Parivarta: the Mahayana doctrine of virtue, which says that merits earned by one's own actions can be used to the advantage of others (*parinamana*).

Parivrajaka (*paribbajaka*): an itinerant, a mendicant monk.

Patra (*patta*): alms bowl.

Phala: the fruit of actions, which can be positive (*punya-karman*) or negative (*papa-karman*).

Pitaka: "basket"; the name of the three collections of the Buddhist canon, the collections of the sayings and actions of the Buddha, meaning the Pali canon. These are the Sutta Pitaka ("Basket of Discourses"); Vinaya Pitaka ("Basket of Monastic Discipline"); and Abhidamma Pitaka ("Basket of Scholastic Doctrine").

Pradaksina (*padakkhina*): "to turn to the right"; the ritual circumambulation around a sacred person or altar.

Prajna (*panna*): awareness, wisdom, supernatural intuition, the highest perfection (*paramita*). In the Mahayana school, it is one of the two essential postulates for achieving enlightenment (*bodhi*), the other being "means" (*upaya*). In the mysticism and iconography of Tibetan Buddhism, *prajna* denotes the female half of the divine couple, together with *upaya*. The term *prajna* is preferable to the term *shakti*, usually used in the West, since *shakti* is not used in Buddhist texts for the name of the god's mate.

Prajnamatra: elements of intelligence or discrimination; the formal elements of art.

Prajnaparamita: the Perfection of Wisdom sutras, which are the base of the Madhyamika school, according to which awareness of emptiness and of the illusory nature of all the minimal elements of physical reality is basic to wisdom, beginning with the five aggregations or components (*skandhas*) and the twelve primary causes (*nidanas*). This concept is personified in the pantheon of Tibetan Buddhism by a goddess about whom much has been written and who has been described and presented as a female bodhisattva. She holds a book in one hand while making a gesture of teaching with the other. She figures among the ten (or twelve) *Paramitas* and also among the ten *Sadhanas*.

Prana: breath; in the Vedic concept, it is a vital spirit related to the cosmic function of the Brahman, and its control is an essential part of the practice of yoga. In Tantric Buddhism it is one (*anapanasmrti*) of the practices in the evolution toward ecstasy.

Pranayama: fourth of the eight steps in astanga yoga, consisting in the control of breathing through appropriate exercises.

Prandihana: the decision by a bodhisattva to act to save as many living things as possible from the bonds of sorrow.

Prapanca (*papanca*): expansion; the apparent state of the illusory world, a result of ignorance.

Pratimoksa (*patimokkha*): the "profession of faith"; the list of 227 sins and penalties recited collectively by Buddhist monks and nuns four times a month during the *upavasatha*.

Pratiti: the awareness of perceiving something. Seeing or intuiting; sensing the style of a work of art.

Pratiyasamutpada (*paticca-samuppada*): the Twelve Links of Conditioned Existence (Twelve Nidanas) that cause continuous rebirths (*samsara*); when eliminated, these make possible the movement toward total extinction (*nirvana*) or enlightenment (*bodhi*). They are ignorance (*avidya*), aggregation (*samskaras*), reflective consciousness (*vijnana*), name-form (*nama-rupa*), the five senses plus the mental (*sadayatana*), contact or perception (*sparsa*), sensation (*vedana*), desire (*trsna*), attachment (*upadana*), existence (*bhava*), birth (*jati*) and old age-death (*jara-marana*).

Pratyahara: the fifth of the eight steps in astanga yoga, it consists in freeing the senses from the dominion of physical objects. It is a practice drawn from various Tantric-Tibetan schools.

Pravrajya (*pabbajja*): "departure"; the abandonment and renouncement of the world by a novice monk (*sramanera*).

Pudgala: an "individual"; according to the first disciples of the Buddha individuals were merely transitory aggregations, but other Buddhist sects see them as actually existing and thus "persons."

Puja: the act of religious worship and part of the individual worship consisting most of all in prayer and in the repetition of prayers with the aid of a rosary.

Punya-skandha (*punya-kandha*): "meritorious portion"; the whole of the positive actions (*punya-karmanta*) that help on the path toward enlightenment.

Purana: the eighteen Vedic texts (six for those who live in ignorance, six for those who live in passion, six for those who live in virtue) which began the knowledge of the Buddha once he left his home; he ordered that their knowledge be overcome.

Purusha: man; a person in the spiritual sense (the term *jiva* is used for the individual sense). The term is used in Buddhism, most of all Tibetan Buddhism, in the sense of "cosmic man," "a spirit of the universe."

R

Raga: passion, greed, desire (also as *raja*), an expression of the thirst for life (*trsna*) and therefore the most serious of the moral afflictions or poisons (*kleshas*). The others (there are usually ten) are hate, delusion, anxiety, heresy, doubt, laziness, arrogance, impudence, insensitivity.

Raja: see Raga. Like *rago-guna* (passion) it is characterized by greed, the thirst for possessions, uncontrollable desires.

Ratnasambhava: "born from a jewel"; one of the five celestial Buddhas, the Jinas. Usually colored yellow in Tibetan art. The five celestial Buddhas are Akshobhya, Amitabha, Amoghasiddha, Ratnasambhava, and Vairochana.

Ratnatraya (*ratanattaya*): the Triple Gem, meaning the Buddha, the Dharma, and the Sangha, which also constitute the Triple Refuge (*sarana*) of the novice monk. Also called *triratna* (*tiratana*).

Rddhi (*iddhi*): powers (magical); ten of these are usually listed, which are obtained over the course of Buddhist training, but the Buddha prohibits their use.

Rsi: a sage; a predominantly Vedic term.

Rupa: "physical body" or natural form, appearance, symbol. It is the world of appearance, most of all the physical world perceptible through forms. It is one of the eighteen spheres of action (*dhatu*) and one of the five components known as *skandhas*. *Buddharupa* is an image of the Buddha.

S

Sadayatana (*salayatana*): the six "containers" of the five senses plus the mental, as applied to their respective spheres of action. There are twelve such containers (*ayatana*), six internal and subjective (*adhyatmika*, *ajjhatida*), involving the five senses and mental perception, and six that are external and are related to the objects of the senses and the things perceived by the mind. *Sadayatana* is the fourth of the twelve primary causes (*nidanas*) of the chain of rebirths.

Sadhana: a successful Tantric practice (a magical practice that brings success to the practitioner). The scope of much of the Sanskrit and Tibetan Buddhist literature of the Greater Vehicle consists in obtaining a favorable action from divinities, both benign and demonic. Sadhanas are thus formulas directed at divinities, whose traits, attributes, and colors must be applied in a specific way.

Sahaja: innate, natural, spontaneous. A result of inclination or will, not force or compulsion.

Saints: Buddhist saints begin with the historical Buddha's first disciples, each of whom became an arhat ("worthy one"): Ananda, Shariputra, and Kashyapa. Both arhats and bodhisattvas perform roles that make them comparable to Buddhist saints; *see also* Siddha.

Sakrdagamin (*sakadagamin*): "he who must return again" and be reincarnated.

Sakti (*Shakti*): power; the female principle; the wife of Siva or some other god; the magical powers (*rddhi*) of the Buddha and the bodhisattvas. In Vajrayana Buddhism, Saktis are female figures, wives of the Tathagata and the bodhisattvas and symbolic of the power of the law of the Dharma, of which they are intrinsic materializations; the preferred term for these beings is *prajna*.

Samadhi: "absorption of the mind," "trance," thus superawareness, ecstasy, "ecstatic meditation." A state of serene quiescence that is reached intuiting the essential truth after acquiring wisdom (*prajna*). The word also refers to the exercises necessary to achieve this paranormal state. It is the last of the eight steps in astanga yoga, corresponding to complete spiritual realization.

Sambhala: mythical kingdom located in a hypothetical north, a sort of celestial Ultima Thule sacred to the tutelary god Kalachakra. In this ideal kingdom the souls of the good are reborn; it is separated from the world by the river Sita. It is probably an idealization of the most remote region of Tibet.

Sambhogakaya: "union body," "celestial body" (from *kaya*, "body"). Existential condition of the bodhisattva before incarnation; the level of awareness in which the bodhisattva exists before incarnation.

Samjna (*sanna*): perceptions, the awareness of phenomena. One of the five components or aggregations known as *skandhas*. The other four are physical form (*rupa*), sensations or feelings (*vedana*), mental constructions or attitudes (*samskaras*), and consciousness (*vijnana*).

Samkhya: philosophical system the Hindu religion says was taught by the avatar (incarnation) Kapila, which was atheistic, based on the analytical study of the spiritual soul and on a purely material conception of the world. It was studied by the Buddha at the beginning of his search for the truth.

Samsara: flux. The cycle of birth, death, and rebirth, hence the transmigration of the self through a series of physical bodies; *samsara* can be brought to an end through the observance of the Dharma and its truths. It is the opposite of nirvana.

Samskara (*sankhara*): mental construction or disposition, an existing attitude; the reality of every existing element perceived as a result of past actions. The second of the twelve *nidanas*. The principal *samskaras* are feeling or sensation (*vedana*), perception (*samjna*), will (*cetana*), focused attention (*ekagrata*), mental visualization of the object (*manasi-kara*), decision (*adhimoksa*), reflection (*vicara*), energy (*virya*), reasoning (*vitarka*), intention (*chanda*), presence of spirit (*smrti*), and intelligence-wisdom (*prajna*).

Samskr: to build, to put together, to perfect; from which *samskrta*, meaning "perfected," the root of the name *Sanskrit*, a language that was built, integrated, and perfected.

Samskrta: aggregated, composed; the condition of the minimal elements of physical reality according to *samskara*.

Sanatana: eternal.

Sangha: the Buddhist community, the order composed of monks (*bhiksu*, *sramana*) and lay members (*upasakas*). It is the third element of the Triple Gems (*ratnatraya*).

Sannyasa: term from the Vedic religion for the renouncement of the fruits of positive actions, the fourth and final step of the spiritual life,

leading to the complete renouncement of the world.

Santi: calm, supreme peace, total extinction, nirvana.

Sastra: text or treatise written by a sage, as distinct from a text based on a revelation (*sruti*), hence a traditional authority.

Satori: the state of sudden enlightenment sought in Zen; such a state can be brief or can continue until the achievement of nirvana.

Satyayuga: the first era in a cycle of four, lasting 1,728,000 years, during which most human beings live in a state of spiritual purity.

Shadaksara: the six syllables that compose the sacred formula "Om ma-ni pad-ma hum" ("the jewel of the lotus"). A formula repeated most of all in honor of the bodhisattva Avalokiteshvara.

Shakyamuni: "the sage of the Shakyas," the name given Siddhartha Gautama (Siddhattha Gotama), the historical Buddha.

Shin: Japanese school of Pure Land Buddhism according who which salvation can be achieved through faith alone.

Shramana (*samana*): Buddhist monk; the feminine is *sramani* (*samani*). A synonym is *bhiksu*.

Shramanera (*samanera*): novice Buddhist monk.

Shunya: the absolute void, emptiness, the absence of all matter. This is the objective reality of the minimal elements of physical reality (the dharmas), which are themselves without substance and which exist for an infinitesimal period of time (*ksana*) on the basis of their reciprocity. In the Zen Buddhist guidelines of art, it is a law of composition, according to which part of every painting, usually the lower right corner, must be "occupied" by emptiness.

Shunyata: emptiness, the condition of *shunya*; the concept transcends the world of preconceived ideas and helps one reach greater awareness. In the Zen Buddhist guidelines of art, a rule of painting holds that the state of emptiness should be part of the composition, balanced with the other portions of the work.

Shunyavada: the profession of emptiness, a theory and name of the Madhyamika school.

Siddha: perfect, accomplished. The state of the yogin or adept who has achieved supreme incorruptibility

(*vajra*) and has reached liberation while still remaining in life. Particularly accomplished or great *siddhas* (*mahasiddhas*) can be considered Buddhist saints.

Siddhi: magical powers possessed by the *siddha*, similar to *rddhi* powers and usually already at a latent state in every human being.

Sila: use, custom, ordinary habit, in particular the five moral precepts for lay members of a community and ten moral precepts for Buddhist monks.

Silpa (*sippa*): art, every work of art, every form of artistic expression, as well as the profession of an art taught by a master (*acarya*).

Simhanada (*sihanada*): "the roar of the lion"; adjective applied to the discourses of the Buddha, in particular the sermon at Benares (Varanasi).

Skandha (*sihanada*): component or aggregation; one of a series of the parts of a whole or a *sela*. The term is used to define the five categories whose association constitutes the transitory relation of the human condition: physical form (*rupa*), sentiments or feelings (*vedana*), perceptions (*samjna*), mental constructions or attitudes (*samskaras*), and consciousness (*vijnana*).

Smasana: the Eight Cemeteries (eight sites of cremation: *astamasana*), an important image in Tibetan mandalas, most of all if located in a circle around an infernal or terrifying divinity. They have proper names and guardian divinities.

Smrti (*sati*): memory, awareness (tradition entrusted to memory); the attention applied to what one is thinking or doing, to an object on which one is concentrating. Also the attention placed on the exercise of *anapanasmrti* breathing or to any similar Buddhist meditation practice. *Smrti*, or *smrtisastra*, is the name of the completion of the Vedas and the Upanishads. In Tibetan Buddhism it is personified by a deity that is one of the four assistants of Mahasarasvati and also one of the eight *yogini*.

Smrtiupasthana (*atipatthana*): the application of *smrti* in the contemplation of the Four Realities: body (*kaya*), sensations (*vedana*), knowledge (*citta*), and the existence of things (*dharma*), which is one of the exercises on the route to enlightenment.

Sopadhisesanirvana
(*savupadisesanibbana*): the first phase of nirvana, in which the five (or ten) moral afflictions, or "fires," are extinguished and enlightenment is reached although substrates of karmic actions remain, to be finally erased in the second phase, or *nirupadhisesanirvana*.

Sparsa (*phassa*): contact, perception; through *sparsa* one perceives the world as something external. It is the sixth of the twelve primary causes (*nidanas*) of the chain of rebirths (*samsara*).

Sri: beauty, prosperity, fortune, light, splendor, wealth, power; the name of an Indian goddess, wife of Vishnu, also called Lakshmi. When incorporated into the pantheon of Tibetan Buddhism she became two different divinities: Sri and Lakshmi. As the wife of Vishnu she is located under the feet of Paramasva, together with Indrani.

Srotapanna (*sotapanna*): a "stream enterer," meaning a novice just beginning on the route toward nirvana.

Sruti: what has been heard, a "revelation," a sacred text (the Vedas); an authority whose value is recognized.

Sthavira (*thera*): "elders"; the name given the Buddha's first disciples and to the Theravada or Hinayana school, which was based on their teachings.

Stupa (*thupa*): a dome-shaped Buddhist memorial mound or shrine, beginning with the funeral monuments erected over the relics of the Buddha, which began as heaps of earth contained within a stone balustrade and later became stone structures, often with decorated walls; Chinese pagodas were based on these structures. The word applies to any shrine holding the ashes of a saint or canonical books. According to their symbolic-emblematic formula, a stupa begins, from above, with the sun, the moon, and thirteen umbrellas alternating with thirteen wheels; there is then the main body, the drum (tall and voluminous), the steps, and the throne of the base.

Sudra: the lowest social class in the *varna* caste division, composed of the subject peoples; it can also be expanded to take in the artisans, farmers, and merchants (the Vaisyas).

Sukhavati: "happy home"; in Tibetan Buddhism, the paradise located to the west that is home to the Amitabha Buddha.

Sutra (*sutta*): literally the thread on which the pages of writings of teachers were strung; a brief discourse, aphorism, or text. In Buddhism the word is used for the "words of the Buddha." The word also applies to the second "basket" of the Pali canon.

Svabhavashunya: something that is empty of its own nature, a term related to absolute reality.

Swami: a Hindu ascetic or religious teacher.

Swastika: a bard who speaks words of welcome or praise; a lucky object; a sign in the shape of a hooked cross made on persons or things as a good-luck charm; a sun symbol found on tablets from the Indus Valley civilization.

T

Tantra: literally "warp," by extension a subject, treatise, or "book"; a collection of the texts of an Indian religion, most of all Hindu or Buddhist scriptures. The Hindu books are esoteric works based on sexual symbolism that demonstrates the duality (positive-negative, male-female) that originated from the division of a primal divinity that created the universe, such that the union of the two opposites repeats the divine act. In Buddhism, the Tantra are works of Tibetan Buddhism based on revelations outside the canon that the Buddha made to various initiates; there are also the works of Adibuddha, of Buddha archetypes, or of bodhisattvas. They follow rules of yoga and Indian Tantrism in terms of the worship of love and sex based on the belief in divine creation as the division into male and female, such that the union of the male and female repeats creation in a symbolic way and inspires divine ecstasy.

Tapasya: austerity. The voluntary acceptance of the restrictions of the world in order to obtain superior benefits, an important concept in Vedic beliefs.

Tara: from *tr*, "to cross, to pass"; she who lets pass, the savior. She is also the star that shows the way. Tara is probably the deification of a Tibetan queen, the wife (actually two wives) of the founder of Lamaism. She is attributed with the power to save those who invoke her help in escaping eight specific dangers: lions, elephants, snakes, fires, bandits, demons, shipwreck, and prison, In Tibetan iconography Tara appears in three versions, as an assistant to Avalokiteshvara; as the sovereign of a mandala or subject of a *sadhana*; as the *prajna* of a Jina. As the sovereign of a mandala she appears as the Green Tara, White Tara, Black Tara, and Yellow Tara (Rasjasri Tara, "the royal woman"; Vajrtara, "the most famous"; Prasanna Tara, the "serene"); the multicolor and multiform Tara; the Tara with indeterminate colors and shapes. As Tara Prajna, fourth of the great *prajnas* (Locana, Mamaki, Pandara, Tara) she is associated with the Jinas of the cardinal points and is paired with Amoghasiddha.

Tariki: Japanese term for the use of the power of others for one's own salvation, as opposed to the use of one's own power.

Tathagata: "the one who has gone before," "he who has gone," "he who has thus come" (also interpreted as "he who follows in the steps of the predecessors"); a name for the Buddha or for a Jina. The Tathagata is a cosmic archetype manifested on the tangible plane of the Dharma (Dharmakaya). The Tathagata emanates bodhisattvas and the Manusi-Buddha.

Tathata: "the being, the essence, the being thus" (*tatha*); the real essence of the world, meaning emptiness, the absolute void (*shunya*), the essence of which is perceptible only to the enlightened.

Thangka (*thanka*): paintings on cloth used as votive hangings, most of all in Buddhist monasteries.

Thera: elder; the first disciples of the Buddha and their school; another form of *Sthavira*.

Theravada: "the Doctrine of the Elders," the school of Buddhism as it was handed down by the first disciples of the Buddha, thus the traditions of the Hinayana, or Lesser Vehicle, school.

Tilak (Sanskrit *tilaka*): a spot of powder or paste (perhaps made using clay from a sacred river) worn on the forehead by Hindu men and women as a religious symbol.

Tretayuga: in Hindu cosmology, the second era (*yuga*) of a cycle of four (*mahayuga*), lasting 1,296,000 years.

Trikaya: "three bodies"; the three modalities or vehicles of manifestation used by the cosmic Buddha; these bodies are the body with which he came to earth (*nirmanakaya*, the "emanation body," the body of the visible, historical body of Siddhartha Gautama); his spiritual body (*sambhogakaya*, or "enjoyment body," "body of bliss," expressing an essential quality or level of awareness of a bodhisattva before incarnation); and his "truth body" (*dharmakaya*): an essential aspect of the Dharma, a specific condition for knowing or preaching the law.

Tripitaka (*Tipitaka*): the "three baskets," the name given the Pali canon of Buddhist texts, which are divided in three parts called baskets (perhaps in reference to the baskets in which palm-leaf manuscripts were formerly stored).

Trsna (*tanha*): "thirst"; the desire that leads to the desire to exist (*bhava*) and to enjoy (*kama*) and to live the nonexistent (*vibhava*).

U

Upadana: attachment, bond, tie; a result of the desire to live, which attaches one to actions and therefore to rebirths. It is the ninth *nidana* of the *pratiyasamutpada*.

Upadanaskanda (*upadanakkhanda*): the whole of what is acquired, the consequence of the thirst for life: birth, disease, death, union with what one does not love, separation from what one loves, the failure to obtain what one wants.

Upadhi: the reasons that force us into existence, or the five categories (*skandhas*) whose association constitutes the transitory reality of the human condition: physical form (*rupa*), sensations or feelings (*vedana*), perceptions (*samjna*), mental constructions or attitudes (*samskaras*), and consciousness (*vijnana*); in addition to these are sexual desire (*kama*) and the *kleshas*, the moral afflictions or poisons that lead to rebirth: greed, hate, delusions, anxiety, heresy, doubt, laziness, arrogance, impudence, and insensitivity. There are finally the consequences of our actions (karma).

Upadhyaya (*upajjhaya*): a guide, the monk responsible for a novice (*sramanera*).

Upadi: material cause, act of receiving, result of actions. The opposite term is *anupadisesa*: the not remaining, the state or condition of *nirupadhisesannibbana*. Not to be confused with the term *upadhi*.

Upanishads: sessions or secret teachings, the Vedic philosophical texts composed between the eighth and fourth centuries BC. They develop the concept of the Brahman-Atman, a basic concept of Vedic thinking. In addition to the eleven (or thirteen) original texts there are several hundred that were added in the post-Vedic period.

Upasaka: a devout, the name given the male lay followers of the Buddhist religious system. Female followers are *upasikas*.

Upavasatha (*uposatha*): the day on which Buddhist monks fast, practice abstinence, and perform the *pratmikosa* ritual, which involves the collective recitation of the 227 sins and their relative punishments; this takes place four times each month at the beginning of the lunar week.

Upaya: the means to achieve an end. In Buddhism, it is the "way" to achieve enlightenment. Most of all in Tibetan Buddhism, it is deified as a figure that represents compassion (*karuna*); it is also the power of every female companion of a Tathagata or a bodhisattva (*sakti*); more generally, it refers to the male element of a divine or mystical couple.

Upaya kaushalya: "skill in means," meaning the ability (of a Buddha or bodhisattva) to adapt his teachings to the surroundings and to the abilities and understanding of the student receiving the message.

Upeksa (*upekkha*): equanimity, a cardinal virtue in Buddhism. The others are benevolence (*maitri*), joy (*mudita*), and compassion (*karuna*), to which is added purity (*a-subha*).

Urna: jewel; the small protuberance on the forehead of the Buddha in some images. It represents the so-called third eye, which sees beyond the material.

Ushnisha: the protuberance on the top of the head of the Buddha in some images. It represents the flame of supreme enlightenment.

V

Vairochana: "enlightener"; the most important of the five celestial Buddhas, the Jinas. Also called Kayesa, Kayesvara, lord of the body, Sasvata (the eternal), and Mahavairochana (Great Vairochana). In Tibetan iconography he can have one face and two hands, one face and four hands, three faces and six hands, four faces and two hands, or four faces and eight hands. The five celestial Buddhas are Akshobhya, Amitabha, Amoghasiddha, Ratnasambhava, and Vairochana.

Vaishakha (*Vesakha*): the Buddhist month (between April and May) during which, on a night of full moon, the birth, enlightenment, and nirvana of the historical Buddha are celebrated. Hence the Buddhist festival called Vesak.

Vaisyas (*Vessa*, *Vesiyana*): the third caste in the social hierarchy established by the Aryan invaders of India. The Aryans established four castes: priests (Brahmans); warriors or nobles (Ksatriyas); artisans, farmers, and merchants (Vaisyas), and the subject people (Sudras).

Vajra: lightning, thunderbolt, diamond. In Tibetan Buddhism it is the symbol of *tathata*, the essence of the absolute emptiness of the world (*sunya*), which is perceptible only to the enlightened. It is represented as an object, usually made of bronze, with a handle that unites two pairs of spokes. In the Tibetan pantheon there are sixteen Vajra divinities, comparable to the figures of the bodhisattvas.

Vajradhatu: the sphere of lightning, the formless level on which awareness of the material void (*sunya*) is created.

Vajrasattva: the essence of lightning. A theological figure in the Mahayana school, symbolic of the absolute and incorruptible condition that is present in every human being.

Vajrayana: the Diamond-Thunderbolt Vehicle; the school of esoteric "visualization" based on the union of mystical concepts from Tibetan Buddhism with the philosophy of Indian Tantrism, directed at making each human being aware of his or her *vajrasattva* potential.

Varana: wall, barrier, obstacle, as, for example, prejudice, which acts as an obstacle to revelation and thus to enlightenment.

Varuna: Hindu divinity incorporated into the pantheon of Tibetan Buddhism. A sky god and one of the principal divinities of Vedic India, he was the first of the sons of Aditi known as the Adityas. In Hinduism he is the guardian of the West; also called Nagavajra or Samudra.

Vasana: latent memory of past experiences; personality; the psychic conditioning that leads to the compulsion to repeat and copy past actions. Also identification, empathy, creative sensibility; but also degrading emotional associations, the force of habit.

Veda: knowledge; the four sacred tests of the Brahman religion, compiled between 2000 and 1200 BC and divided into four books, the Rig-Veda (hymnology; *rig* means "stanza of praise"); the Sama-Veda (*saman* means "chant, melody"); the Yajur-veda (from *yajus*, "sacrificial prayer"); and the Atharva-Veda (the *atharvan* were the priests involved in fire worship, which along with sacrifice was at the base of the Brahman religion). The most important is the first, which contains the cosmological hymns that served as the basis of philosophical concepts throughout India.

Vedana: sentiments or feelings, the whole of the six senses, the five physical plus the mental. It is one of the five *skandhas*, the term used for the five components or aggregates that when put together constitute the transitory reality of the human condition. The other four are physical form (*rupa*), perceptions (*samjna*), mental constructions or attitudes (*samskaras*), and consciousness (*vijnana*).

Vesak: name of the principal Buddhist festival; *see* Vaisakha.

Vibhuti: that which penetrates, pervades; abundance, power; development, multiplication, a manifestation of power.

Vidya (*vijja*): knowledge, one of the ten stages of spiritual attainment (*bhumi*); synonymous with *jnana*. When the knowledge is "superior" it becomes mystical knowledge, or *prajna*.

Vihara: residence, retreat; the Buddhist monastery. The word is also applied to a spiritual state.

Vijnana (*vinnana*): "consciousness," the entity that is reincarnated; reflective consciousness, the psychic form that leads to individual awareness and thanks to which the individual can follow the Eightfold Path: right faith, right will, right speech, right action, right livelihood, right effort, right mindfulness, and right concentration (*ashtanga-marga*). *Vijnana* is the last and most important of the five components or aggregations (*skandhas*); the other four are physical form (*rupa*), perceptions (*samjna*), mental constructions or attitudes (*samskaras*), and consciousness

(*vijnana*). Synonyms include mind (*manas*), intellect (*buddhi*), and awareness (*citta*). The most important consciousness container is the *alaya-vijnana*.

Vikalpa: concepts, images. The "imagination" that creates the psychic personality (*vasana*) composed of the tendency to repeat and copy certain past actions.

Vinaya: the rule, monastic discipline; name of the first basket of the Pali canon (Vinaya Pitaka: "Basket of Monastic Discipline").

Vipashyana (*vipassana*): insight as a result of meditation, the result of exercises and the practice of meditation that reveal previous errors and lead to greater awareness of the transitory nature of existence and of the minimal elements of reality (the dharmas).

Virya (*viriya*): vigor; one of the *paramitas*, the six or ten stages of spiritual attainment or perfection (*bhumi*) that the bodhisattva must develop in order to achieve enlightenment. The others are generosity, or liberation from the thirst for possessions (*dana*); morality (*sila*); patience (*ksanti*); meditation (*dhyana*), and wisdom of reality (*prajna*).

Vishnu: the omnipotent, the immanent. A divinity found throughout India and integrated into the Tibetan Buddhist pantheon. In the Rig-Veda he has great importance as a sun god and as an ally of Indra; later, in Hinduism, he holds a place of importance in a triad with Brahma and Siva. He appears on earth under various guises or incarnations (avatars). In the Tibetan pantheon he is the guardian of the Eastern gate.

W

Wabi: Japanese term for the state of mental serenity. It is the ideological basis of Japanese art and culture.

Wat: A Thai Buddhist temple or monastery.

Y

Yaksha: divinity-spirits common to Indian religious systems and assimilated into Buddhism along with their king, Kubera, god of wealth and guardian of the North. Although sometimes presented in grotesque form, they tend to be benevolent spirits and dispense wealth to humans.

Yama: personification of death; also

called Vajrakala, Antaka, Vaivasvata. A Hindu divinity incorporated into the pantheon of Tibetan Buddhism. Four ferocious female divinities have names that begin with Yama, and they are located at the far corners of a mandala: Yamadahi, black and yellow, to the southeast; Yamaduti, yellow and red, to the southwest; Yamadamstri, red and green, to the northwest; and Yamamathani, green and black, to the northeast.

Yana: vehicle, calling, route; the word appears in such names as Mahayana, Hinayana, Navayana.

Yantra: a magic diagram, a means, something intricate, thus a symbolic representation, by way of a geometric design, of a concept or a divinity. The sacred diagram of Tantric Hinduism known as the Shri yantra is important to India; it is composed of a series of overlapping triangles, half pointing downward, half pointing upward.

Yoga: literally "yoking," "subjecting," thus "union with the absolute." Yoga is a group of spiritual disciplines directed at the attainment of full self-realization. Jnana yoga is based on knowledge; karma yoga on action; hatha yoga on physical exercise used to reach a mystical state. Bhakti yoga (or Buddhi-yoga), the path of love—perhaps the highest expression of yoga—is taught in the Bhagavad-Gita. The basic text of yoga is the Yoga Sutras of Patanjali, which dates to the second century BC. Yoga has been a part of Buddhism since its origin.

Yogi or yogin: a person who practices yoga.

Yogini: a kind of goddess or witch of Hindu mythology. Incorporated into the pantheon of Tantric Buddhism, they became the companions of yogis in mystical-erotic rites. There are a great many kinds of yogini, with different names and grouped into different categories as satellite divinities; as such they often populate the large mandalas of Tibetan Buddhism.

Yuga: one of the four (Satya, Treta, Dvapara, and Kali) or eight epochs into which an era (*kalpa*) is divided.

Z

Zen: one of the principal schools of Japanese Buddhism (Ch'an in Chinese), based on sudden enlightenment achieved through an approach to reality using formulas that overcome reason and rise above or break through normal thinking processes.

Bibliography

Anesaka, Masaharu. *Buddhist Art in Its Relation to Buddhist Ideals*. New York: Houghton Mifflin, 1915.

Asvaghosa. *Buddhacarita*. Saranath, Varanasi: Central Institute of Higher Tibetan Studies, 1995.

Bary, William Theodore de, ed. *The Buddhist Tradition in India, China, & Japan*. New York: The Modern Library, 1969.

Bechert, Heinz, and Richard Gombrich, eds. *The World of Buddhism*. London: Thames and Hudson, 1984.

Bhattacharyya, Benoytosh. *Indian Buddhist Iconography*. Calcutta: Firma K. L. Mukhopadhyay, 1968.

Bloch, J., J. Filliozat, L. Renou. *Canon. Bouddhique Pali*. Paris: Maisonneuve, 1989.

Carrithers, Michael. *The Buddha*. Oxford: Oxford University Press, 1983.

Coomaraswamy, Ananda K. *Elements of Buddhist Iconography*. Cambridge, MA: Harvard University Press, 1935.

------. *History of Indian and Indonesian Art*. New York: E. Weyhe, 1927.

------. *Yakshas*. New York: Oxford University Press, 1993.

Conze, Edward, trans. and ed. *Buddhist Wisdom*. New York: Vintage Books, 2001.

Dagyab, Loden Sherap. *Tibetan Religious Art* (2 vols). Wiesbaden: Harrassowitz, 1977.

Dalai Lama XIV. *My Land and My People*. London: Weidenfeld & Nicolson, 1962.

------. *An Introduction to Buddhism*. New Delhi: Tibet House, 1965.

Dasgupta, S. N. *Hindu Mysticism*. Delhi: Motilal Banarsidass, 1992.

Fisher, Robert E. *Buddhist Art and Architecture*. New York: Thames and Hudson, 1993.

Harris, Elizabeth J. *What Buddhists Believe*. Oxford: One World Publications, 1998.

Harvey, Peter. *An Introduction to Buddhism: Teachings, History, and Practices*. New York: Cambridge University Press, 1990.

Karetzky, Patricia E. *The Life of the Buddha*. Lanham, MD: University Press of America, 1992.

Keown, Damien. *Buddhism: A Very Short Introduction*. New York: Oxford University Press, 2000.

Lamotte, Étienne. *History of Indian Buddhism*. Louvain-la-Neuve: Institut Orientaliste, 1988.

Malalasekera, G. P., et al., eds. *Encyclopedia of Buddhism*. Colombo: Government of Sri Lanka, 1961.

Menzies, Jackie, ed. *Buddha: Radiant Awakening*. Sydney: Art Gallery of New South Wales, 2002.

Olschak, B. C., and G. T. Wangyal. *Mystic Art of Ancient Tibet*. London: Allen & Unwin, 1973.

Ross, Nancy Wilson. *Buddhism: A Way of Life and Thought*. New York: Vintage Books, 1981.

Trainor, Kevin, ed. *Buddhism: The Illustrated Guide*. New York: Oxford University Press, 2004.

Tucci, Giuseppe. *The Theory and Practice of the Mandala*. New York: S. Weiser, 1970.

---. *Tibetan Painted Scrolls*. Rome: Libreria dello Stato, 1949.

Zwalf, W., ed. *Buddhism—Art and Faith*. London: British Museum Publications, 1985.

Credits

The photographs in this book are from the collection of the author, with the following exceptions: Maraja (Verona, Italy), pages 34, 50, 51, 58r, 59, 62–63a, 62b, 75, 77, 96, 100b, 102, 103, 106, 107, 109b, 112; the Nasli and Alice Heeramaneck Collection, pages 70, 73, 108, 109; the Shelley and Donald Rubin Foundation Collection: 110.